My First Dictionary

Published 2018 by The Gresham Publishing Company Ltd.,
Academy Park, Building 4000, Gower Street,
Glasgow, G51 1PR, Scotland,
United Kingdom

Copyright © 2018 The Gresham Publishing Company Ltd.

All rights reserved. No part of this publication may be reproduced, stored in a retrieval system or transmitted in any form or by any means, electronic, mechanical, photocopying, recording or otherwise, without the prior permission of the publisher.

Conditions of Sale: This book is sold with the condition that it will not, by way of trade or otherwise, be resold, hired out, lent, or otherwise distributed or circulated in any form or style of binding or cover other than that in which it is published and without the same conditions being imposed on the subsequent purchaser.

ISBN 978-1-85534-030-5

Artwork in this book is copyright ©: Mimi Everett; courtesy of Shutterstock: 3d_man, Absent A, Aleksangel, alekseyk, Alfazet Chronicles, Alhovik, Andrew Rybalko, aninata, ANNA ZASIMOVA, Astrovector, Barashkova Natalia, BigMouse, Bildagentur Zoonar GmbH, BlueRingMedia, Bonezboyz, brgfx, BVA, By owatta, Christos Georghiou, ConceptCafe, cosmaa, Creative Mood, d1sk, dashadima, deymos, Dmitry Natashin, Dotted Yeti, DRogatnev, Dzianis_Rakhuba, Eisfrei, Enmaler, Everilda, Fuga, gladcov, Golden Sikorka, goldyg, GraphicsRF, graphixmania, GreyLilac, Hennadii H, Iamnee, Iconic Bestiary, ILeysen, insima, Ivan_Nikulin, IvanC7, jagoda, Jo karen, Julia August, Julia Musdotter, Jorgen Mus, Julianna Million, Kachurivski, Kiarnight, kontur-vid, Ku_suriuri, ladyfortune, laraslk, Ledelena, Leigh Prather, Light-Dew, Lorelyn Medina, Lorri Kajenna, Loulouka1, M.Stasy, Macrovector, Marish, Maxx-Studio, miha de, Mingirov Yuriy, MoreVector, Mr. Chuckles, MSSA, Murina Natalia, mything, NaDo_Krasivo, Nature Art, Natykach Nataliia, nikiteev_konstantin, nosorogUA, olegtoka, Oleksiy Mark, Osiv, Peter Hermes Furian, Phoebe Yu, PYRAMIS, Ricardo Romero, sababa66, Sabelskaya, Sarawut Padungkwan, Sasha Ka, Sedova Elena, Shirstok, siridhata, Sk Elena, SkyPics Studio, SofiaV, Spreadthesign, StockSmartStart, studioworkstock, subarashii21, Sudowoodo, Sundra, Sundry Studio, Sunny_nsk, sweetok, Tancha, Telnov Oleksii, Tetiana Yurchenko, Thomas Soellner, tynyuk, Uranium, Usagi-P, varuna, Vasif Maharov, Vector Tradition, Vectorpocket, VectorShow, VicW, Viktor Manko, viktoriya_art, Vitaliy Snitovets, yavi, Yayayoyo, YevO, Yurumi, zizar, Zonda, Zvereva Iana.

Contents

About This Dictionary	iii
A Guide to the Dictionary	iv
The Dictionary at a Glance	vi

About This Dictionary

My First Dictionary is a dictionary for early learners aged 5+. Designed to get them engaged with language at an early age, *My First Dictionary* is a step beyond a simple picture dictionary. It introduces language at an appropriate level, increasing young learners' word power and helping them to develop some of the skills they will need to become good readers. Almost 1,000 familiar words are each defined in a full sentence, with a helpful example sentence showing the word being used.

With its colourful and fun illustrations and bright design, *My First Dictionary* is intended as an interactive resource for use by teachers or parents with their children. Read each entry together: help the children to recognise the appearance of the individual letters of the alphabet, see how they are arranged, and how they sound. The first letter of each headword has been highlighted in red for this purpose.

Some of the headwords in this dictionary are made up of simple sounds that learners may already recognise, others are words which children will meet in their environment, such as the names of animals or words that describe the weather, and so on.

Talk about the subject matter of each entry with the learners. Information on a variety of topics can be found within the definitions and their example sentences, providing an opportunity for further learning. For a more detailed description of the features in this dictionary, see pages iv–vi.

A Guide to the Dictionary

With your help as a teacher or a parent, this dictionary is an excellent tool to help young learners find out what a word means and how to use it, as well as how to spell it correctly. A clear and user-friendly layout helps to make the entries in *My First Dictionary* accessible to learners, and the illustrations are intended to help them understand the meaning of a word. They will get to know some of the most commonly used English words.

Working through this dictionary with learners will help them to pick up and use some of the skills they need to become good readers on their own, such as how to use pictures to decode words, and how to recognise the individual letters of the alphabet, sound them out and combine them.

To support teachers, parents and learners, each part of this dictionary is described in more detail below. Some suggestions are given for possible activities.

HEADWORD

accident *noun*

The **headword** is what we call the word in bold letters at the beginning of each entry in this dictionary. This is the word that is explained by the **definition** (see page v). The headwords in this book are listed in **alphabetical order**, following the order of the letters that appear in the English alphabet from A to Z. The alphabet is shown down the side of each page of the dictionary.

Sometimes the more familiar form of a headword is used, to suit the younger reader, but the longer form of the word is still included in brackets. For example, 'case' is used as the headword but 'suitcase' appears in brackets after 'case'.

case (suitcase) *noun*

The first letter of each headword is a red letter. Draw the learner's attention to this. Let learners look for more examples of this letter among the words that follow in the entry and in that letter's section of the dictionary. Look at the other letters in the headword and help learners to sound them out. When the headword is a simple short word of three or four letters like 'act' and 'ant', ask the learners to try and sound out the individual letters and put them together to make the headword.

PARTS OF SPEECH

Most of the headwords in this dictionary are followed by one of the four main parts of speech (noun, verb, adjective and adverb) in grey letters. The part of speech tells you what kind of word the headword is and what it does.

bark *noun*

Is the headword a naming word? A **noun** is the name given to a word that names a person, thing or quality.

Is the headword a doing word? A **verb** is the name given to the word in a sentence that tells us what someone or something (a noun) is doing. You cannot make a proper sentence without a verb.

Does the headword describe something more about a noun? **Adjective** is the name given to words that tell us more about a noun (for example its colour, size, quantity or quality). Adjectives describe nouns.

Does the headword describe how something is being done? **Adverb** is the name given to words that tell us more about how something is being done. Adverbs describe verbs. They often (but not always) end in '-ly'.

The parts of speech mentioned in this dictionary are the basic building blocks of our language and while children at this level do not need to be too concerned about them and their function, their presence in grey letters is one way of introducing the idea that different words do different things.

DEFINITION

> **accident** *noun*
> An **accident** is when something bad happens that is not planned or done on purpose.

The **definition** of a word is a sentence that tells you what the word means. The headword is highlighted in bold letters in the sentence. Read the headwords and their definitions with learners. To make sure your learners understand what a headword means, encourage them to talk about its definition and its illustration if there is one.

NUMBERED DEFINITIONS

Headwords that look and sound the same and share the same part of speech can sometimes have several very different meanings. In this dictionary, any different definitions like this are included in the same entry under the headword but they are numbered and given a new line as you can see in the example below.

> **bark** *noun*
> **1** A **bark** is the short sharp sound that a dog and some other animals make.
> *Our dog has a very loud **bark**.*
> **2 Bark** is also the name of the hard outside covering of the trunk and branches of a tree.
> *The **bark** of a tree provides a home for many insects and spiders.*

Headwords that look and sound the same but are not the same kind of words – that is, they have different parts of speech – are included in this dictionary as separate entries with a superscript numeral next to each headword, as shown below.

> **can¹** *verb*
> If you **can** do something, you are able to do it.
> *I had some swimming lessons and now I **can** swim.*
>
> **can²** *noun*
> A **can** is a metal container for storing food, drinks or paint.
> *We needed two **cans** of paint when we painted our garden fence.*

EXAMPLE SENTENCE

> *Our dog has a very loud **bark**.*

Each headword definition is followed by an example sentence that shows the headword being used in context. The headword appears in bold letters in the example sentence. Some example sentences also include information about animals and food and other topics.

Read an **example sentence** with the learner and make sure they understand it. Then encourage them to make up a sentence of their own about the headword. Learners can draw a picture that illustrates the example sentence. Some example sentences provide an opportunity to talk about the topic of the sentence and possibly link it to other classroom activities.

ILLUSTRATIONS

The colour illustrations in this dictionary are there to support the text and help young learners to understand what a word means.

They can be used to encourage learners to talk about what they see, or to share any other knowledge they may have about the headword represented by the illustration. An illustration can also encourage the learners to make their own pictures of the headword.

The Dictionary at a Glance

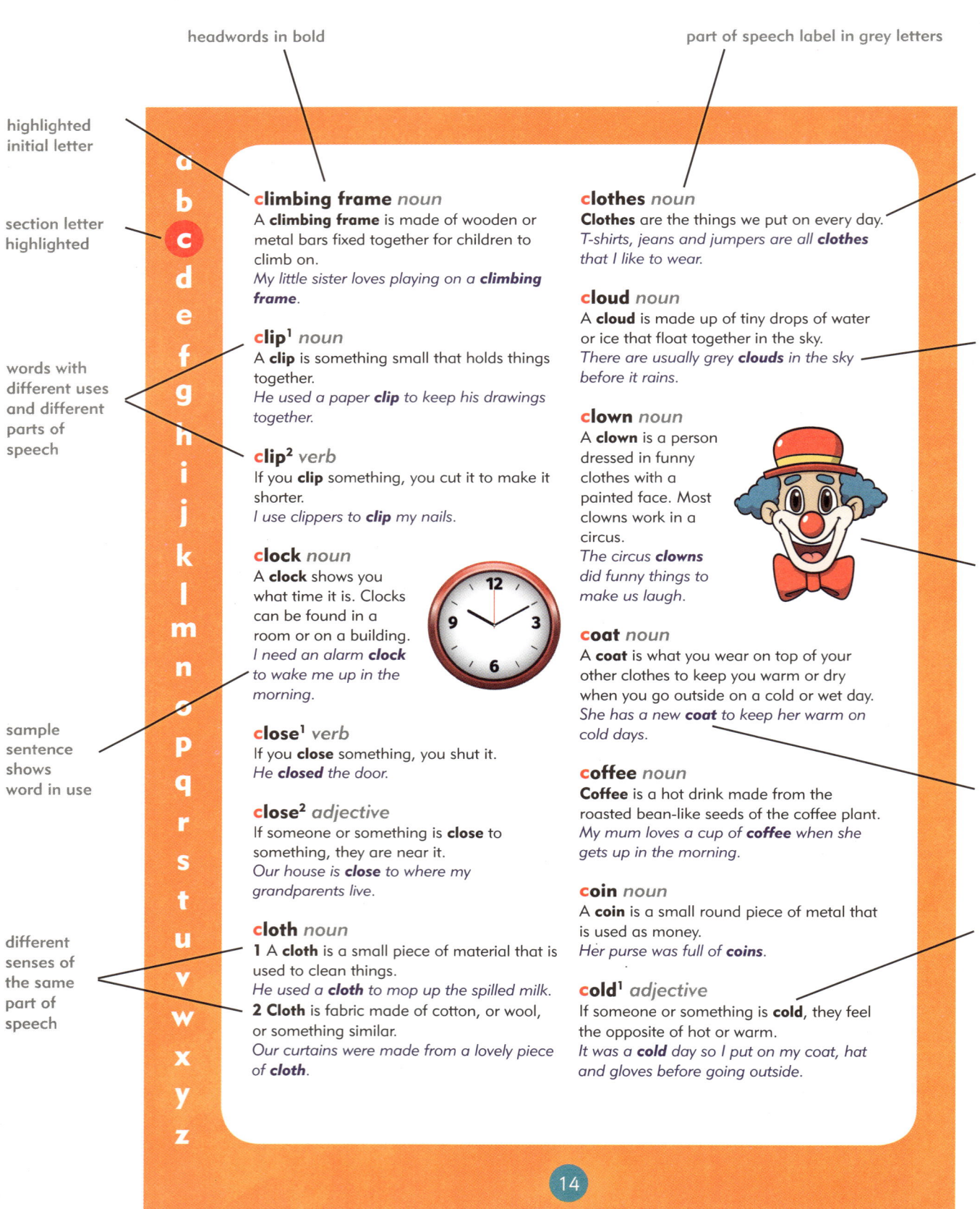

- highlighted initial letter
- section letter highlighted
- words with different uses and different parts of speech
- sample sentence shows word in use
- different senses of the same part of speech
- headwords in bold
- part of speech label in grey letters
- definition written as a sentence
- informative example sentences
- pictures illustrate definitions
- headword highlighted in bold in the example sentence
- headword highlighted in bold in the definition

climbing frame *noun*
A **climbing frame** is made of wooden or metal bars fixed together for children to climb on.
*My little sister loves playing on a **climbing frame**.*

clip¹ *noun*
A **clip** is something small that holds things together.
*He used a paper **clip** to keep his drawings together.*

clip² *verb*
If you **clip** something, you cut it to make it shorter.
*I use clippers to **clip** my nails.*

clock *noun*
A **clock** shows you what time it is. Clocks can be found in a room or on a building.
*I need an alarm **clock** to wake me up in the morning.*

close¹ *verb*
If you **close** something, you shut it.
*He **closed** the door.*

close² *adjective*
If someone or something is **close** to something, they are near it.
*Our house is **close** to where my grandparents live.*

cloth *noun*
1 A **cloth** is a small piece of material that is used to clean things.
*He used a **cloth** to mop up the spilled milk.*
2 **Cloth** is fabric made of cotton, or wool, or something similar.
*Our curtains were made from a lovely piece of **cloth**.*

clothes *noun*
Clothes are the things we put on every day.
*T-shirts, jeans and jumpers are all **clothes** that I like to wear.*

cloud *noun*
A **cloud** is made up of tiny drops of water or ice that float together in the sky.
*There are usually grey **clouds** in the sky before it rains.*

clown *noun*
A **clown** is a person dressed in funny clothes with a painted face. Most clowns work in a circus.
*The circus **clowns** did funny things to make us laugh.*

coat *noun*
A **coat** is what you wear on top of your other clothes to keep you warm or dry when you go outside on a cold or wet day.
*She has a new **coat** to keep her warm on cold days.*

coffee *noun*
Coffee is a hot drink made from the roasted bean-like seeds of the coffee plant.
*My mum loves a cup of **coffee** when she gets up in the morning.*

coin *noun*
A **coin** is a small round piece of metal that is used as money.
*Her purse was full of **coins**.*

cold¹ *adjective*
If someone or something is **cold**, they feel the opposite of hot or warm.
*It was a **cold** day so I put on my coat, hat and gloves before going outside.*

Aa

accident *noun*
An **accident** is when something bad happens that is not planned or done on purpose.
*He did not mean to break the plate – it was an **accident**.*

act *verb*
1 To **act** is to do something.
*You need to **act** quickly if something goes on fire.*
2 If you **act** in a play, you pretend to be someone else.
*She is going to **act** as a nurse in her school play.*

address *noun*
Your **address** is the name or number of the house, the street, and the town or village where you live.
*My aunt put my **address** on the parcel she sent for my birthday.*

adventure *noun*
An **adventure** is something exciting you do or that happens to you.
*Travelling by plane is an **adventure**.*

aeroplane *see* **plane**

afternoon *noun*
The **afternoon** is the part of the day between 12 o'clock in the middle of the day and 6 o'clock in the evening.
*I left home late in the morning and got to town in the **afternoon**.*

age *noun*
1 Your **age** is the number of years you have lived.
*What **age** will you be on your next birthday?*
2 An **age** is a special time in history.
*In the Stone **Age**, people made tools from stone.*

air *noun*
The **air** is the mixture of gases we breathe. Air surrounds the earth.
*We went outside for some fresh **air**.*

aircraft *noun*
An **aircraft** is a machine that can go up in the air and move through it.
*Planes and helicopters are **aircraft**.*

airport *noun*
An **airport** is a place where planes take off and come in to land.
*We arrived at the **airport** in plenty of time to catch our plane.*

alarm *noun*
An **alarm** is a noise or a signal that tells people something is wrong.
*The fire **alarm** went off and we had go outside.*

alien *noun*
In some stories and films an **alien** is a person or a creature from another world.
*An **alien** came out of the spaceship.*

all

1 You use **all** to mean the whole of something.
*She can eat some of the cake but not **all** of it.*
2 You can also use **all** to mean everyone or everything.
***All** of the children were working very hard.*

alligator noun

An **alligator** is a large reptile that looks a bit like a crocodile. It has a long body and a flat tail.
***Alligators** live in freshwater ponds, rivers, lakes and swamps.*

alphabet noun

The **alphabet** is all the letters that are used in a language to make words.
*The letters of the English **alphabet** are written in a special order.*

always adverb

1 If you **always** do something, you do it every time or on a regular basis.
*My mum **always** goes shopping on a Friday.*
2 Always can also mean forever.
*I will **always** love my little sister.*

ambulance noun

An **ambulance** is a vehicle that takes people who are hurt or ill to hospital.
*The **ambulance** went quickly to the road accident.*

anchor noun

An **anchor** is a kind of heavy metal hook fixed to a ship with a long chain. When an anchor is dropped into the sea, it holds the ship in place and stops it from moving.
*The ship's captain ordered his crew to lower the **anchor** into the sea.*

angry adjective

If you are **angry**, you are cross and feel very upset.
*He was **angry** because someone had taken his book without asking.*

animal noun

An **animal** is a living thing that is not a plant or a person.
*There are lots of wild **animals** in Africa.*

ankle noun

Your **ankle** is the part of your body that joins your leg to your foot.
*He broke his **ankle** when he fell from the tree.*

ant noun

An **ant** is a small insect that lives with other ants in an ant colony.
*The **ants** lived in an anthill made of earth and sand.*

apple noun

An **apple** is the round fruit of the apple tree.
*Most **apples** are sweet to eat and very good for you.*

apron noun

An **apron** is clothing that you wear over the front of your clothes, and tie at the back, to keep your clothes clean when cooking or doing messy jobs.
*She wears an **apron** when she is baking a cake.*

area noun
An **area** is a part of a town, or a country, or the world.
*We live in an **area** that has many forests.*

arm noun
Your **arm** is the part of your body between your shoulder and your hand.
*The girl raised her **arm** and waved.*

arrow noun
1 An **arrow** is a long, thin, straight stick with a sharp point at one end that is aimed at a target and shot from a bow.
*Someone who shoots an **arrow** from a bow is called an archer.*
2 An **arrow** can also be a sign shaped like this → that shows people where to go.
*Follow the **arrows** until you reach the exit.*

art noun
Art is the name given to painting, drawing and sculpture.
*She loves going to her **art** lessons.*

ask verb
1 When you **ask** someone about something, you are saying something to them in order to get an answer or some information.
*'What are you doing after school?' she **asked**.*
2 When you **ask** someone for something, you are saying to them that you want them to do something or give you something.
*She **asked** her mum for some sweets.*

asleep adjective
When you are **asleep**, you are sleeping with your eyes closed and your mind and body resting.
*She was **asleep** before her bedtime story was finished.*

assembly noun
An **assembly** is a group of people meeting together in one place for the same reason.
*They had a school **assembly** every morning.*

assistant noun
1 An **assistant** is someone who helps someone else with their work.
*The manager asked her **assistant** to make a list of the jobs to be done that week.*
2 An **assistant** is someone whose job is to help you.
*My mum asked the shop **assistant** to help her find a new hat.*

astronaut noun
An **astronaut** is a person who is trained to travel in a spaceship.
*The **astronaut** went for a space walk.*

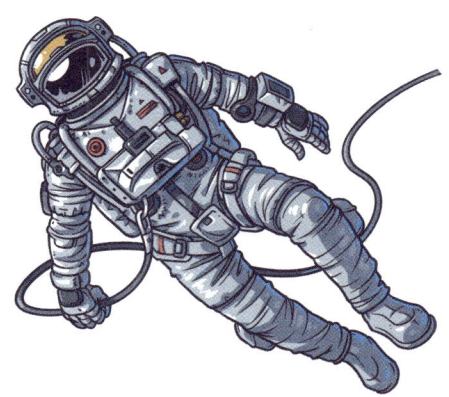

athlete noun
An **athlete** is a person who is very good at sports such as running.
*Lots of **athletes** take part in the Olympic Games.*

atlas noun
An **atlas** is a book of maps.
*She used her **atlas** to find out where New York City is.*

aunt noun
Your **aunt** is the sister of your mother or father, or your uncle's wife.
*The little girl went to stay with her **aunt**.*

autumn *noun*
Autumn is the season between summer and winter.
*In some countries, trees lose their leaves in **autumn**.*

awake *adjective*
If you are **awake**, you are not sleeping.
*She was **awake** most of the night with a sore tummy.*

away *adverb*
1 If someone or something is **away**, they are somewhere else.
*She is **away** on holiday with her mum and dad.*
2 If you put something **away**, you place it where it should be, in its usual place.
*He put his toys **away** in the toy box.*

awful *adjective*
If something is **awful**, it is very bad or unpleasant.
*He wore the same socks for a week and they smelled **awful**!*

Bb

baby *noun*
A **baby** is a very young child that cannot walk or talk yet.
*The **baby** cried because he was hungry.*

back *noun*
1 Your **back** goes from your neck to your bottom on the opposite side of your body to your chest and stomach.
*She likes to float on her **back** in the swimming pool.*
2 The **back** of something is the side or part of it that is farthest from its front.
*We like to play in the garden at the **back** of our house.*

bacteria *noun*
Bacteria are very small creatures that can only be seen under a microscope. Some bacteria are good and some are harmful.
*The **bacteria** in yogurt are good for us.*

bad *adjective*
If we say someone or something is **bad**, we mean they are not good.
*The **bad** boy pushed his little sister off her bike.*

badge *noun*
A **badge** is a small piece of metal, plastic or cloth with a design or words on it.
*I pinned the **badge** on my jacket.*

bag *noun*
A **bag** is a container made of cloth, leather, plastic or paper. A bag is used to carry or hold things.
*At the baker's shop they put our bread into a paper **bag**.*

4

ball noun
1 A **ball** is an object that is completely round.
*The **ball** rolled down the hill.*
2 You use a **ball** in many different games and sports.
*She hit the tennis **ball** very hard.*

balloon noun
A **balloon** is a small coloured bag made of thin rubber that you fill with air then use as a decoration or as a toy.
*The little girl had lots of pink **balloons** at her birthday party.*

banana noun
A **banana** is a long curved fruit with soft sweet flesh and a thick yellow skin.
***Banana** trees grow best in hot countries.*

bang noun
A **bang** is a sudden loud noise.
*When the wind blew the door shut, there was a loud **bang**.*

bark noun
1 A **bark** is the short sharp sound that a dog and some other animals make.
*Our dog has a very loud **bark**.*
2 **Bark** is also the name of the hard outside covering of the trunk and branches of a tree.
*The **bark** of a tree provides a home for many insects and spiders.*

basket noun
A **basket** is a container made of thin strips of wood or cane with a handle. It is used to carry or hold things.
*My neighbour always carries her shopping in a **basket**.*

bat noun
1 A **bat** is a specially shaped piece of wood with a handle that is used to hit the ball in games like cricket or baseball.
*My dad showed me how to hold a cricket **bat**.*
2 A **bat** is a small animal with wings that hunts for its food at night.
*A **bat**'s wings are made of skin not feathers.*

bath noun
A **bath** is a long deep container for holding water, in which you can sit and wash yourself all over.
*They have a **bath** and a shower in their bathroom.*

bathroom noun
A **bathroom** is a room with a bath or a shower, and often it also has a wash-hand basin and a toilet.
*In our house the **bathroom** is next to my bedroom.*

beach noun
A **beach** is the narrow part of land next to the sea, covered in sand or pebbles.
*The fisherman pulled his boat up onto the **beach**.*

bear noun
A **bear** is a large, heavy wild animal with a thick fur coat and sharp claws.
***Bears** have a very good sense of smell.*

bed noun
A **bed** is a piece of furniture that you lie down on to sleep or rest.
*I need a new mattress for my **bed**.*

bedroom noun
A **bedroom** is a room with a bed in it where you sleep.
*She shares her **bedroom** with her sister.*

bee noun
A **bee** is a small flying insect that makes honey and beeswax.
***Bees** live in a hive and they can sting you if they get angry.*

beetle noun
A **beetle** is an insect with four wings and a hard shell-like covering for its body.
*Many **beetles** are beautifully coloured.*

bell noun
1 A **bell** is a piece of metal shaped like a cup that makes a ringing noise when something hits it.
*Can you hear the school **bell** ringing?*
2 A **bell** is also something that makes a ringing noise as a kind of signal or warning.
*Use your bicycle **bell** to warn people you are coming.*

belt noun
A **belt** is a long narrow strip of material, such as leather or plastic, that fastens around your waist.
*He wore a black **belt** to hold his trousers up.*

best adjective
If you say someone or something is the **best**, you mean that they are better than all the others.
*He is the **best** footballer in his team.*

bike (bicycle) noun
A **bike** is vehicle with two wheels, two pedals to make the wheels turn, a saddle to sit on and handlebars to steer with.
*I ride my **bike** to school every day.*

big adjective
1 If something is **big**, it is large in size.
*The elephant is a very **big** animal.*
2 If you have a **big** sister or a big brother, you have a sister or brother who is older than you.
*She has a **big** brother and a little sister.*

bin noun
A **bin** is a container for your rubbish.
*We have four large rubbish **bins** – one for food, one for plastic and glass, one for paper and cardboard, and one for general rubbish.*

bird noun
A **bird** is an animal with feathers, wings and a beak.
*Baby **birds** hatch from eggs.*

birthday noun
Your **birthday** is a celebration of the day you were born. It happens every year on the same day.
*She had a wonderful party on her **birthday**.*

biscuit noun
A **biscuit** is a kind of small, flat, crisp cake.
*He likes chocolate **biscuits**.*

bit noun
If you have a **bit** of something, you have a small piece of it.
*He gave me a **bit** of his chocolate bar.*

bite noun
1 A **bite** is what happens when you cut into something using your teeth.
*She ate a hot dog in three big **bites**.*
2 A **bite** is also a sore place where something, such as an insect, has bitten you.
*She had a nasty insect **bite** on her arm.*

black adjective
If something is **black**, it is the colour of the sky at night.
*Thick **black** smoke came from the burning building.*

blackboard see **chalkboard**

blanket noun
A **blanket** is a large piece of soft material that is used as a covering to keep people warm.
*She had a lovely woollen **blanket** on her bed.*

blue adjective
If something is **blue**, it is the colour of the sky on a sunny day.
*She was wearing **blue** shorts and a white T-shirt.*

boat noun
A **boat** is a small open vehicle for travelling on water that is moved by using oars, sails or an engine.
*A **boat** with an engine is called a motor boat.*

body noun
The word **body** describes all of the parts, inside and out, that make up a person, but not their mind.
*You can keep your **body** fit and well by exercising every day.*

book noun
A **book** is made up of pieces of printed paper, with words or pictures on them, inside a cover.
*She was given a **book** of stories for her birthday.*

boot noun
1 A **boot** is a kind of shoe that covers the whole foot and part of the leg.
*She needed new winter **boots**.*
2 A **boot** is also the space at the back of a car for luggage and other things.
*He helped his mum put the shopping in the **boot** of the car.*

bottle noun
A **bottle** is a container for keeping liquids in. It is made of glass or plastic with a narrow neck and a lid.
*She carefully poured the lemonade from its **bottle** into her cup.*

bottom noun
1 The **bottom** of something is its lowest part.
*He walked down to the **bottom** of the hill.*
2 Your **bottom** is the back part of your body below your waist and above your legs.
*She slipped on the muddy path and fell on her **bottom**.*

bowl noun
A **bowl** is a round deep dish used to hold fruit or salad. It is also used in baking when mixing foods such as flour, sugar, butter and eggs.
*There were three **bowls** of different sizes in the kitchen cupboard.*

box noun
A **box** is a kind of container with straight sides and a lid. Boxes are often made of cardboard or wood. A box can be used for keeping things in or for sending things in the mail.
*My mum got a **box** of chocolates on her birthday.*

boy noun
A **boy** is a male child or young person.
*When he was a **boy**, he lived on a farm with his mum and dad.*

bread noun
Bread is a common food made with flour and baked in an oven.
*She loves **bread** and butter with jam.*

break verb
If you **break** something, it falls to pieces or stops working.
*If you drop that glass, it will **break** into pieces.*

breakfast noun
Breakfast is the first meal of the day.
*He had cereal for **breakfast**.*

bridge noun
A **bridge** is a structure built over a river, a road or a railway so that people and vehicles can cross from one side to the other.
*They have built a new wooden **bridge** over the river.*

bring verb
If you **bring** something with you to a place, you have it with you when you come.
*Mum says she will **bring** some bottles of water in case we get thirsty.*

brother noun
Your **brother** is a boy or man who has the same parents as you.
*He has three **brothers**.*

brown adjective
If something is **brown**, it is the colour of chocolate or dark wood.
*She has beautiful **brown** eyes.*

brush noun
A **brush** has a handle and strong short hairs or bristles at one end. It is mainly used for cleaning.
*She swept the floor with a **brush**.*

bubble noun
A **bubble** is a small ball of gas or air inside a very thin layer of liquid.
*She loves lots of **bubbles** in her bath.*

bucket noun
A **bucket** is a metal or plastic container with a handle. Buckets are used for holding or carrying water.
*The cleaner uses a **bucket** of hot soapy water to wash the floor.*

budgie (budgerigar) noun
A **budgie** is a small yellow and green parakeet with a long tail that eats seeds and is often kept as a pet.
*I have two pet **budgies**.*

bug noun
1 A **bug** is a small insect.
*The roses in my garden are covered in little green **bugs**.*
2 A **bug** is also a kind of illness caused by a virus or bacteria.
*He was off school for a week with a tummy **bug**.*

building noun
A **building** is something that has been built with walls, windows and a roof.
*A house, a factory and a block of flats are all **buildings**.*

bull noun
A **bull** is a grown-up male calf.
*The farmer bought a new **bull** at the cattle sale.*

bump verb
If you **bump** something, you knock into it suddenly.
*I **bumped** my knee against the chair.*

burn verb
1 If you **burn** something, you set it on fire.
*We **burn** coal and wood in our fireplace to keep the house warm.*
2 If you touch something very hot, you will **burn** yourself.
*I touched the hot iron by mistake and **burned** my hand.*

bus noun
A **bus** is a large motor vehicle with seats for people who pay to be taken from one place to another by road.
*She is travelling by **bus** to see her aunt.*

busy adjective
If you are **busy**, you have lots of things to do.
*I was very **busy** all day.*

butter noun
Butter is a soft, yellow food made from cream that is used as a spread and in cooking.
*He loves **butter** on his bread.*

butterfly noun
A **butterfly** is a kind of insect with a long body and four large wings.
***Butterflies** are busy during the day, feeding on the sweet nectar produced by flowers.*

button¹ noun
A **button** is small round object made of metal or plastic. It is pushed through a buttonhole to fasten together clothes like shirts.
*The **button** came off my shirt and I had to sew it back on.*

button² verb
If you **button** up clothes, you fasten them together with buttons.
*He **buttoned** up his shirt.*

buy verb
If you **buy** something, you hand over money to pay for it.
*We went to the shops to **buy** some new clothes.*

buzz noun
A **buzz** is a low humming sound like the one that flying bees make when they beat their wings together.
*The **buzz** of the bees made me feel sleepy.*

Cc

cage *noun*
A **cage** is a container or a room with bars where animals or birds are kept.
*They put the lions in a **cage** and moved them by lorry to a new animal park.*

cake *noun*
A **cake** is a kind of sweet food (made from flour, fat, eggs and sugar) that is baked in an oven.
*I made a birthday **cake** for my dad.*

calculator *noun*
A **calculator** is a small machine that helps you to do sums.
*My brother took his **calculator** to school.*

calendar *noun*
A **calendar** gives a list of all the days, weeks, months and special dates in the year.
*We looked at a **calendar** to see what day of the week my birthday is on this year.*

calf *noun*
A **calf** is a young cow or a young bull.
*The **calf** was calling for its mother.*

call *verb*
1 When you **call** someone something, you give them a name.
*We **call** our cat Ginger because it is orange.*
2 When you **call** out, you shout or cry out.
*She had to **call** out for help when she fell.*

camel *noun*
A **camel** is a big four-legged animal with a long neck and one, or two, humps on its back. Camels live in the desert.
***Camels** are used to carry people or things in the desert.*

camera *noun*
A **camera** is a device that is used to take photos.
*I took some photos with my new **camera**.*

can¹ *verb*
If you **can** do something, you are able to do it.
*I had some swimming lessons and now I **can** swim.*

can² *noun*
A **can** is a metal container for storing food, drinks or liquids.
*We needed two **cans** of paint when we painted our garden fence.*

candle *noun*
A **candle** is a stick of wax with a piece of string called a wick running through it. When you light a candle, it gives off light.
*When the electricity went off during the storm, we used **candles** to see in the dark.*

canoe *noun*
A **canoe** is a small narrow kind of boat. People move a canoe through the water using paddles.
*She paddled the **canoe** quickly through the water.*

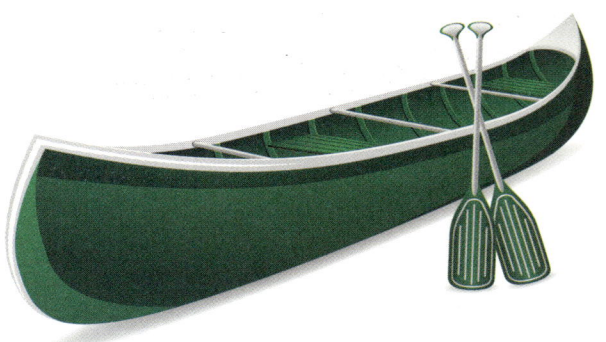

10

cap noun
A **cap** is a small, soft hat with a bit that sticks out at the front.
*He lost his favourite baseball **cap**.*

car noun
A **car** is a vehicle with four wheels that is moved by an engine and is used to carry people from place to place.
*Their **car** has four doors.*

card noun
1 **Card** is a kind of stiff paper.
*The children cut different shapes out of coloured **card**.*
2 A **card** is a folded piece of thick paper with a picture on the outside and a message inside.
*She got lots of **cards** on her birthday.*

cardboard noun
Cardboard is a very strong stiff paper that is used to make boxes.
*We used lots of big boxes made of **cardboard** when we moved house.*

carpet noun
A **carpet** is a kind of soft thick floor covering often made from wool.
*He tripped and spilled his glass of milk on the **carpet**.*

carrot noun
A **carrot** is a long orange vegetable that grows under the ground.
*I like eating **carrots** and peas.*

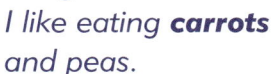

carton noun
A **carton** is a cardboard or plastic container in which food or drink is sometimes sold.
*There is a **carton** of orange juice in the fridge.*

cartoon noun
1 A **cartoon** is a drawing that tells a very short story or a joke.
*My dad laughed at the funny **cartoon** in the newspaper.*
2 A **cartoon** is a film where thousands of drawings are made to look like they are moving.
*The children love to watch **cartoons** on TV.*

case (suitcase) noun
A **case** is a kind of container with a handle. A suitcase is used for carrying things.
*I packed my **case** because I was going to stay with friends.*

castle noun
A **castle** is a large building with high thick walls built long ago to keep people safe from attack by their enemies.
*Hundreds of soldiers attacked the **castle**.*

cat noun
A **cat** is a small four-legged animal with soft fur that is kept as a pet or for catching mice.
*Our **cat** has very sharp claws.*

catch verb
1 If you **catch** something, you take hold of it while it is moving.
*She tried to **catch** the ball while it was in the air.*
2 If you **catch** a train (or a bus or a plane), you go to a train station (or a bus station or an airport) and get on a train (or a bus or a plane).
*We arrived at the train station just in time to **catch** our train.*

caterpillar *noun*
A **caterpillar** is a small animal that looks a bit like a worm. A caterpillar turns into a butterfly or a moth.
*Most **caterpillars** eat green leaves and grow very quickly.*

CD (compact disc) *noun*
A **CD** is a round flat piece of plastic with music or information on it.
*The library has a large collection of **CDs**.*

cereal *noun*
Cereal is a breakfast food made from grains such as wheat or oats.
*I have a bowl of **cereal** and milk every morning before I go to school.*

chair *noun*
A **chair** is a seat for one person that has four legs and a back to lean on.
*They moved some **chairs** into the school hall for the children to sit on.*

chalk *noun*
Chalk is a soft white rock that can be made into small sticks for writing on a chalkboard.
*The teacher wrote out a sum on the board using **chalk**.*

chalkboard *noun*
A **chalkboard** is a wooden board, painted black, on which you write with chalk. **Blackboard** is another name for a chalkboard.
*The teacher wrote some more sums on the **chalkboard**.*

cheek *noun*
Your **cheek** is one of the two parts of your face below your eyes and on either side of your nose.
*She cried when her friend went away and tears ran down her **cheeks**.*

cheese *noun*
Cheese is a solid food made from milk. Some **cheeses** are hard and some are soft and creamy.
*She put some **cheese** in the pasta sauce.*

cherry *noun*
A **cherry** is the small fruit of the cherry tree. It is round, soft and red with a hard seed stone in the middle.
*Be careful not to choke on the stone inside a **cherry**!*

chest *noun*
1 Your **chest** is the part of your body between your neck and your waist.
*The strong man has a broad **chest**.*
2 A **chest** is also a large box with a lid.
*The wooden **chest** was full of blankets.*

chick *noun*
A **chick** is a baby bird or baby chicken that has just hatched.
*The hen's **chicks** were covered in soft yellow feathers.*

chicken *noun*
A **chicken** is a young hen that people keep for its eggs and its meat.
*Our **chickens** lay lots of eggs.*

child *noun*
1 A **child** is a boy or girl before they grow into a young adult.
*I learned how to ride a bike when I was a **child**.*
2 A **child** is also someone's son or daughter.
*Our neighbours only have one **child**.*

chin *noun*
Your **chin** is the part of your face below your mouth.
*He hurt his **chin** when he fell off his bike.*

chip noun
A **chip** is a very small piece that has been broken off, or cut off something.
*The plate had a **chip** on the edge.*

chocolate noun
Chocolate is a sweet brown food made from cocoa beans, milk and sugar.
*I got a bar of **chocolate** as a treat.*

cinema noun
A **cinema** is a place where people go to watch films.
*My mum took my brother and me to the **cinema** to see a film.*

circle noun
A **circle** is a round shape like a ring.
*The teacher asked us to draw a **circle** and colour it in.*

circus noun
A **circus** is a kind of show where acrobats, clowns and trained animals do their acts in a big tent.
*She enjoyed watching the acrobats and the strongman at the **circus**.*

city noun
A **city** is a large or important town.
*The roads going into the **city** were very busy.*

clap verb
If you **clap** your hands, you hit your hands together to make a loud noise over and over again.
*Everyone **clapped** to show how much they had enjoyed the concert.*

class noun
A **class** is a group of people who learn things together.
*I am the tallest child in our **class**.*

classroom noun
A **classroom** is a room in a school where a class of children have their lessons.
*Our **classroom** is bright and sunny.*

claw noun
A **claw** is one of the sharp curved nails on the foot of a bird or an animal.
*The cat scratched my leg with its **claws**.*

clean adjective
If something is **clean**, it has no dirt or stains on it.
*I put on **clean** clothes after a shower.*

clever adjective
If someone is **clever**, they learn and understand things quickly and easily.
*There are some very **clever** children in my class.*

climb verb
When you **climb**, you go up towards the top of something, sometimes using your hands and feet.
*He **climbed** the tree, right up to the top.*

cling verb
If you **cling** to someone or something, you hold on to them tightly.
*The little boy **clings** to his mum when they are at the shops.*

climbing frame noun
A **climbing frame** is made of wooden or metal bars fixed together for children to climb on.
*My little sister loves playing on a **climbing frame**.*

clip¹ noun
A **clip** is something small that holds things together.
*He used a paper **clip** to keep his drawings together.*

clip² verb
If you **clip** something, you cut it to make it shorter.
*I use clippers to **clip** my nails.*

clock noun
A **clock** shows you what time it is. Clocks can be found in a room or on a building.
*I use an alarm **clock** to wake me up in the morning.*

close¹ verb
If you **close** something, you shut it.
*He **closed** the door.*

close² adjective
If someone or something is **close** to something, they are near it.
*Our house is **close** to where my grandparents live.*

cloth noun
1 A **cloth** is a small piece of material that is used to clean things.
*He used a **cloth** to mop up the spilled milk.*
2 **Cloth** is fabric made of cotton, or wool, or something similar.
*Our curtains were made from a lovely piece of **cloth**.*

clothes noun
Clothes are the things we put on every day.
*T-shirts, jeans and jumpers are all **clothes** that I like to wear.*

cloud noun
A **cloud** is made up of tiny drops of water or ice that float together in the sky.
*There are usually grey **clouds** in the sky before it rains.*

clown noun
A **clown** is a person dressed in funny clothes with a painted face. Most clowns work in a circus.
*The circus **clowns** did funny things to make us laugh.*

coat noun
A **coat** is what you wear on top of your other clothes to keep you warm or dry when you go outside on a cold or wet day.
*She has a new **coat** to keep her warm on cold days.*

coffee noun
Coffee is a hot drink made from the roasted bean-like seeds of the coffee plant.
*My mum loves a cup of **coffee** when she gets up in the morning.*

coin noun
A **coin** is a small round piece of metal that is used as money.
*Her purse was full of **coins**.*

cold¹ adjective
If someone or something is **cold**, they feel the opposite of hot or warm.
*It was a **cold** day so I put on my coat, hat and gloves before going outside.*

cold² noun
A **cold** is an illness that makes you sneeze and cough.
*She didn't go to school because she had a bad **cold**.*

colour noun
You see the **colour** of an object. Colours have names such as red, blue, yellow, green and purple. Red, blue and yellow can be mixed to match any of the other colours, for example red and yellow mixed together make orange.
*The **colour** of the sky on a rainy day is grey.*

comb noun
A **comb** is a strip of plastic, metal or wood with a row of narrow pointed teeth. You use a comb to style your hair.
*She carries a **comb** in her bag.*

come verb
If you **come** to somewhere, you move towards it or into it.
*He **comes** to my house every day.*

comic noun
A **comic** is a kind of magazine that tells a story in pictures.
*He loves reading **comics**.*

compact disc see **CD**

computer noun
A **computer** is a machine with a screen, mouse and a keyboard. We use computers to find, process and store information.
*We learn about **computers** at school.*

cone noun
A **cone** is a solid shape that is round at the bottom and pointed at the top.
*You can eat ice cream in a crisp wafer that is shaped like a **cone**.*

container noun
A **container** is something that holds things inside it. You can keep things in a container.
*Boxes and bottles are kinds of **container**.*

cook verb
When you **cook** something, you heat it up and make it ready to eat.
*My dad **cooked** some rice for our dinner.*

cooker noun
A **cooker** is a piece of kitchen equipment that is used to cook food.
*Be careful! Some parts of a **cooker** can get very hot.*

cool adjective
1 If you use **cool** to describe something, it can mean it is almost, but not quite, cold.
*It was a **cool** evening after a very hot day.*
2 **Cool** can also mean something is very good or nice.
*'I like your jacket – it is really **cool**!'*

correct adjective
If something or someone is **correct**, they are telling the truth and not making a mistake.
*The **correct** time is 10 o'clock.*

cot noun
A **cot** is a small bed with high sides for a baby or young child.
*The baby is asleep in his **cot**.*

cotton noun
Cotton is a light material made from the soft white fibres around the seeds of the cotton plant.
*My T-shirt is made of **cotton**.*

cotton wool noun
Cotton wool is soft white fluffy cotton. Sometimes it is shaped into balls.
*My big sister takes off her make-up using **cotton wool**.*

cough verb
When you **cough**, you make a loud noise as you force air from your throat. You cough if you are choking or have a bad cold.
*I **coughed** a lot during the night.*

count verb
1 When you **count**, you name the numbers one after the other in the correct order, starting with number 1.
*The little girl can **count** up to 20.*
2 When you **count** things or people, you are working out how many of them there are in a group.
*The teacher **counted** the children and saw that one child was missing.*

cousin noun
Your **cousin** is the son or daughter of your uncle or aunt.
*I love playing with my **cousins** when they come to visit.*

cow noun
A **cow** is a large four-legged female animal that is kept on a farm for its milk.
*The farmer had a field full of **cows**.*

crab noun
A **crab** is a small sea creature with five pairs of legs and a hard shell.
*We found some **crabs** in rock pools at the seashore.*

crane noun
1 A **crane** is a large tall machine with a long arm for moving heavy things.
***Cranes** are used to unload large things from ships.*
2 A **crane** is also a large bird with long legs, a long neck and a long bill.
***Cranes** build floating nests in shallow water.*

crash noun
1 A **crash** is a sudden loud noise like the sound of something breaking or hitting another object.
*The box fell to the floor with a loud **crash**.*
2 A **crash** is also a bad accident caused by two or more vehicles hitting each other hard.
*Two people were hurt in a bad car **crash** near our house.*

crawl verb
To **crawl** is to move forwards on your hands and knees.
*His baby sister is beginning to **crawl**.*

crayon noun
A **crayon** is a short coloured stick made of wax for drawing.
*She used some **crayons** to draw a picture for her mum.*

creature noun
A **creature** is any living thing that is not a plant.
*There are lots of different **creatures** in the world.*

cricket noun
1 **Cricket** is a bat-and-ball game for two teams where players run up and down to score runs. The team that scores the most runs wins.
*There are eleven players in a **cricket** team.*
2 A cricket is a jumping insect that makes a short sharp sound called a chirp.
*We could hear the **crickets** chirping in the long grass.*

crisps noun
Crisps are a snack food and most are made up of thin slices of potato that have been deep-fried or baked until crunchy.
*In some countries, potato **crisps** are called potato **chips**.*

crocodile noun
A **crocodile** is a large reptile with a long tail and scaly body. Crocodiles live mainly in fresh water and feed on fish, other reptiles, birds and animals.
*There was a **crocodile** lying by the river.*

cross¹ noun
A **cross** looks like the letter X.
*We marked our place on the map with a **cross**.*

cross² verb
If you **cross** something, you move from one side of it to the other.
*We **crossed** the busy road after looking both ways.*

cross³ adjective
If you are **cross**, you feel angry about something.
*I was **cross** because my brother pushed me out of the way.*

crow noun
A **crow** is a medium-to-large bird with black or black-and-grey feathers.
*There are many kinds of **crow** in the world.*

crowd noun
A **crowd** is a lot of people all together in one place.
*There was a huge **crowd** waiting to get into the football stadium.*

crown noun
A **crown** is an object, made of gold and decorated with jewels, in the shape of a circle that is worn on the head by a king or queen.
*The king did not wear his **crown** very often.*

cry verb
You **cry** when you are sad or in pain. Tears run from your eyes and down your cheeks when you are crying.
*He fell in the playground and began to **cry**.*

cub noun
A **cub** is the name given to a lot of baby animals including the young of lions, bears, wolves and foxes.
*There were four lion **cubs** playing in the shade of a tree.*

cucumber noun
A **cucumber** is a long green vegetable that is eaten raw in salads.
*She carefully cut the **cucumber** into thin slices.*

cup noun
A **cup** is a small round container, usually with a handle, from which we drink liquids such as tea or coffee.
*I like a **cup** of tea with my breakfast.*

cupboard noun
A **cupboard** is a piece of furniture with shelves and a door, in which we keep things like clothes or dishes.
*We keep our pots and pans in a **cupboard** in the kitchen.*

curly adjective
If your hair is **curly**, it is not straight but has lots of small curves.
*My cousin has blonde **curly** hair.*

curtain noun
A **curtain** is a large piece of cloth that is hung in front of a window to make a room dark or shade it from the sun.
*I open my **curtains** in the morning.*

cushion noun
A **cushion** is a kind of small pillow filled with soft things like feathers. You use a cushion to make a chair more comfortable.
*Our chairs are padded with **cushions**.*

cut¹ verb
1 If you **cut** something, you remove it from a larger piece using something sharp like scissors.
*He **cut** the wrapping paper in half to make a small parcel.*
2 If you **cut** a cake, you use a knife to divide it into pieces.
*I **cut** the cake into eight pieces.*

cut² noun
A **cut** is a sore place where your skin has been opened by something sharp.
*I have a deep **cut** on my arm.*

cymbal noun
A **cymbal** is a round metal plate that is used as a musical instrument. It makes a loud ringing noise when it is banged against another cymbal.
*I played the **cymbals** when we were making music in our classroom.*

Dd

daffodil *noun*
A **daffodil** is a bright yellow flower with a trumpet-shaped centre and a long stem.
Daffodils start to appear in early spring.

daisy *noun*
A **daisy** is a small wild flower with a yellow centre and white petals.
The field was covered in daisies.

damp *adjective*
If something is **damp**, it is a little wet.
The washing on the line is still damp.

dance *verb*
When you **dance**, you move your feet and body to music.
My little sister loves to dance to the music on the radio.

dark *adjective*
When it is **dark**, there is very little light.
Because it was a very dark night, we had to use a torch to see where we were going.

date *noun*
The **date** is the time in terms of the day, month and year when something happens.
The date when my brother was born was 24 March 2018.

daughter *noun*
A **daughter** is the girl child of a mother and father.
Our neighbours have two daughters and a son.

dawn *noun*
Dawn is the time of day when the sun rises.
The birds began to sing at dawn.

day *noun*
1 **Day** is the time between sunrise and sunset when it is light.
It rained all day.
2 A **day** is also a period of time equal to 24 hours.
A day begins at 12 o'clock one night and ends at 12 o'clock the next night.

dead *adjective*
When a person, an animal or a plant is **dead**, they are no longer alive.
I forgot to water the plants and now they are all dead.

deaf *adjective*
If someone is **deaf**, they cannot hear any sounds or they are not able to hear very well.
He is deaf but he knows how to read lips and sign language.

deep *adjective*
If something is **deep**, it goes a long way down from the top.
There is a deep well in their village.

deer *noun*
A **deer** is a medium-sized wild animal that eats grass or leaves. Male deer have antlers.
We saw a deer in the fields near our house.

dentist noun
A **dentist** looks after your teeth if they need to be fixed.
*She went to the **dentist** because she had a sore tooth.*

desk noun
A **desk** is kind of small table, often with drawers. You sit at a desk when you have something to write.
*After a snack, he sat at his **desk** to do his homework.*

device noun
A **device**, especially one that is electrical, is something that is made in order to do a particular job.
*An iron is a **device** for smoothing the wrinkles out of clothing.*

diamond noun
A **diamond** is a very hard and sparkly precious stone.
*Her aunt has a gold ring with one large **diamond**.*

dice noun
Dice are small cubes with a different number of spots (from one to six) on each of their six sides.
***Dice** are thrown in pairs in lots of board games.*

dictionary noun
A **dictionary** is a book or a place online (on the internet) that tells you what words mean.
*She had to look up the words she didn't know in a **dictionary**.*

dig verb
When you **dig**, you break up or remove soil using a spade.
*They had to **dig** some big holes for their new trees.*

digger noun
A **digger** is a big machine that is used to move large amounts of earth.
*He loved watching the **diggers** at work.*

dinner noun
Dinner is the main meal of the day. It can be eaten in the middle of the day or in the evening.
*We had chicken curry for **dinner**.*

dinosaur noun
Dinosaurs were very large reptiles that lived millions of years ago.
*Some **dinosaurs** were small and some were very big.*

dirty adjective
If something is **dirty**, it is not clean and needs to be washed.
*His clothes were always **dirty** after playing football.*

dish noun
A **dish** is a container used for cooking or for holding food.
*She cooked the apple pie in a round **dish**.*

dishes, the noun
The dishes are all the things that people use when preparing, serving and eating a meal.
*We washed all **the dishes**.*

do verb
When you **do** something, you spend time working on it.
*First **do** your homework and then you can go out to play.*

doctor noun
A **doctor** takes care of you when you are sick or hurt.
*The **doctor** said I must rest in bed for a few days.*

dog noun
A **dog** is a four-legged animal that barks.
*Lots of people keep **dogs** as pets.*

doll noun
A **doll** is a toy that looks like a little girl or a baby.
*She got a baby **doll** for her birthday.*

dolphin noun
A **dolphin** is a sea animal that belongs to the whale family.
Dolphins like to swim in a group known as a pod.

donkey noun
A **donkey** is a kind of small horse with long ears that is used to carry things and people.
Donkeys are mainly used as working animals.

door noun
A **door** is usually made of wood and it is used to enter or leave a room, or a building, or a vehicle. It can be opened or shut using a handle.
*Our front **door** is blue.*

down adverb
When something moves **down**, it moves from a higher place to a lower place.
*The rain ran **down** the windowpane.*

dragon noun
Dragons are not real animals. They are found only in stories. They are large creatures that can fly and breathe fire.
*He loved to read stories about **dragons**.*

dragonfly noun
A **dragonfly** is an insect with a long thin body and two pairs of wings that you can see through. Some dragonflies are brightly coloured.
*We saw some **dragonflies** near the pond.*

draw verb
When you **draw**, you use a pencil or crayons to make a picture on paper.
*She likes to **draw** flowers and the sun.*

drawer noun
A **drawer** is like a box without a lid. Drawers slide in and out of other pieces of furniture such as desks or chests of drawers.
*He took a knife and fork out of one of the kitchen **drawers**.*

dream noun
A **dream** is a series of thoughts, pictures and feelings that you have in your mind while you are sleeping.
*I had a funny **dream** about flying like a bird.*

dress noun
A **dress** is a piece of clothing with a top and a skirt joined together.
*She has a pretty blue **dress**.*

drink¹ verb
When you **drink** a liquid, you take it into your mouth and swallow it.
*People **drink** a lot of water when it is hot.*

drink² noun
A **drink** is a liquid that you swallow.
***Drinks** with a lot of sugar in them are bad for you.*

drip verb
If something **drips**, it falls in little drops.
*Water began to **drip** from the tap.*

drive verb
When you **drive** a vehicle, you make it move along in the direction you want to go.
*His big brother is learning to **drive** a car.*

drop¹ verb
If you **drop** something, you let it fall down to the ground.
*She didn't mean to **drop** her glass but it slipped out of her hand.*

drop² noun
A **drop** of something liquid is a very small amount of it.
*He felt a few **drops** of rain and then it stopped.*

drum noun
A **drum** is a round hollow instrument that you hit with your hands or with sticks to make music.
*There was a lot of noise when the **drums** were being played.*

dry adjective
If something is **dry**, it is not wet and it has no water in it or on it.
***Dry** wood burns quickly.*

duck noun
A **duck** is a water bird with short legs and a broad flat bill. **Ducks** have skin between their three front toes (webbed feet). This helps them to swim faster.
*Farmers keep **ducks** for their eggs, their meat and their soft fine feathers called **duck** down.*

dust noun
Dust is a kind of fine dirt that is like powder.
*After the strong winds, there was **dust** all over the inside of our house.*

DVD noun
A **DVD** is a kind of CD that can store lots of music or films.
*I have a **DVD** of my favourite film.*

Ee

ear *noun*
You have one **ear** on each side of your head. Your ears are the two parts of your body that you hear with and that help you to keep your balance.
*His mum took him to the doctor because he had a fever and a very sore **ear**.*

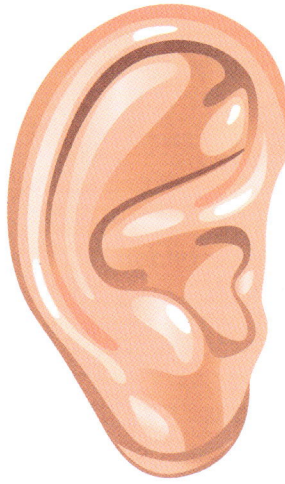

early *adverb*
1 If something happens **early**, it happens before the usual time or the right time.
*We finished school **early** today.*
2 If someone is **early**, they are there before the right time.
*Her baby brother wakes up **early** every day.*

earth *noun*
1 The **earth** (sometimes with a capital letter) is the planet that we live on.
*The **earth** moves round the sun.*
2 **Earth** is another name for the ground or for soil.
*They dug a huge hole and there was **earth** everywhere.*

easy *adjective*
If something is **easy**, it is not hard or difficult to do.
*The spelling test was **easy**.*

eat *verb*
When you **eat**, you put food in your mouth, chew it and then swallow it.
*She loves to **eat** fruit.*

egg *noun*
1 An **egg** is a small oval object with a thin hard shell that is laid by a hen and cooked and eaten by people.
*They had boiled **eggs** for breakfast.*
2 Birds, fish and reptiles lay **eggs**, from which their young ones hatch.
*The turtle lays her **eggs** in the sand.*

elbow *noun*
Your **elbow** is the middle part of your arm where it bends.
*The boy fell off his scooter and hurt his **elbow**.*

elephant *noun*
An **elephant** is a very big grey animal with large ears and two long teeth called tusks. It eats plants using its long nose called a trunk.
*I watched a programme on TV about **elephants**.*

email *noun*
An **email** is a written message or letter sent from one person to another using a computer or mobile phone.
*I got an **email** from my friend in Australia.*

empty *adjective*
If something is **empty**, there is nothing inside it.
*The sweet jar is **empty** – someone has eaten all the sweets!*

end noun
The **end** of something is the last part of it.
*He read the book to its **end**.*

engine noun
1 An **engine** is a machine that makes things work or move using some kind of fuel or power.
*Cars and planes have **engines**.*

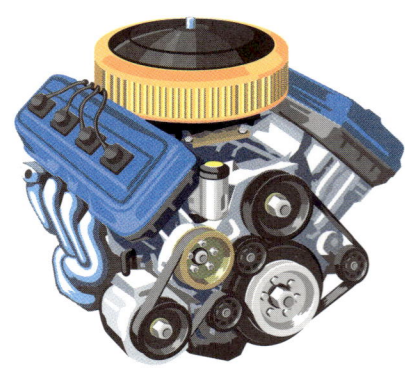

2 An **engine** is also the part of a train that pulls the rest of the train.
*I would love to ride in the **engine** with the driver.*

enormous adjective
If something is **enormous**, it is very very large.
*Russia is an **enormous** country.*

envelope noun
An **envelope** is a folded paper container for a letter.
*He wrote his aunt's name and address on the **envelope**.*

even adjective
If a number is **even** it can be divided by two with nothing left over.
*The numbers two, four, six and eight are **even** numbers.*

evening noun
Evening is the part of day between the afternoon and the night.
*My brother gets home from work at 6 o'clock in the **evening**.*

event noun
An **event** is something important that happens or takes place.
*We are going to a sporting **event** next week.*

ever adverb
You use **ever** to mean at any time.
*Nobody **ever** goes there.*

every adjective
You use **every** to mean all the people or things in a group.
***Every** child in the class works hard.*

excited adjective
If you are **excited**, you are very happy because something good is going to happen and you can't stop thinking about it.
*I am very **excited** about going to the zoo.*

exciting adjective
If something is **exciting**, it makes you feel very happy.
*I have something **exciting** to tell you.*

exercise noun
When you do some sort of **exercise**, such as running or swimming, you are doing something that is hard work. Exercise helps to keep your body healthy.
*Walking to school is good **exercise**!*

expected adjective
If someone is **expected**, there is a good chance they will arrive.
*She was **expected** that evening.*

eye noun
Your **eye** is one of the two parts of your face that you see with.
*'Close your **eyes** and go to sleep!' said my mum.*

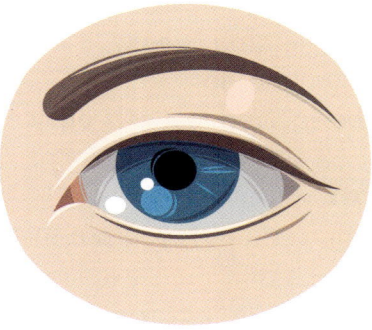

Ff

fabric noun
Fabric is another word for cloth. Fabric is what clothes and things like curtains are made from.
*The **fabric** for my new bedroom curtains has flowers on it.*

face noun
Your **face** is the front part of your head that has your eyes, nose and mouth on it.
*She has a lovely **face**.*

fair¹ adjective
1 If someone is **fair**, their skin and hair are pale or light in colour.
*One sister is **fair** and the other is dark.*
2 If something is **fair**, it is quite good.
*He had done a **fair** job of tidying his room.*
3 If something is **fair**, it follows the rules.
*Two against one is not a **fair** fight.*
4 If the weather is **fair**, it is clear and sunny.
*The weather forecast says we are in for a spell of **fair** weather.*

fair² noun
A travelling **fair** is a number of roundabouts and sideshows that go from place to place. They are set up outside in a public place for people to enjoy.
*Did you have a good time at the **fair**?*

fairy noun
In stories, a **fairy** is a tiny person with wings who can do magic.
***Fairies** look after plants and flowers.*

fall verb
When you **fall**, you drop down suddenly to the ground.
*The path is very slippery – be careful or you will **fall**!*

family noun
A **family** is a group of people living together. A family is often made up of a mother and a father and their children but it can also include grandparents, aunts and uncles and others.
*My **family** is made up of me and my sister, my mum and my grandma.*

famous adjective
If you are **famous**, lots of people know about you.
*She is a **famous** film star.*

fan noun
1 A **fan** is an electric device with blades that move the air around.
*The **fan** helped to cool the hot air.*

2 A hand **fan** made from folded paper or card can also be moved up and down in front of your face to make some cool air.
*She made her own paper **fan** and using it made her feel much cooler.*
3 A **fan** is someone who has a great love for someone or something.
*My sister is a big **fan** of adventure stories.*

farm noun
A **farm** is a place in the country with buildings and fields where people keep animals and grow crops.
*There was a large herd of cattle on the **farm**.*

farmer noun
A **farmer** is a person who owns or rents a farm in order to keep animals and grow crops.
The **farmer** has sheep and cattle on his farm.

fast[1] adjective
1 If something or someone is **fast**, they can move very quickly.
They had two **fast** runners in their team.
2 If a watch or a clock is **fast**, they show a time that is later than the correct time.
His watch is ten minutes **fast**, so instead of 3 o'clock it shows 10 minutes past 3 o'clock.

fast[2] adverb
If someone or something is moving **fast**, they are moving very quickly.
His racing car was moving **fast** through the other cars in the race.

fat adjective
If a person or an animal is **fat**, they weigh too much and this is not good for them.
Being **fat** can lead to illness.

father (dad, daddy) noun
A **father** is a man who has a child or children.
Father and son are both very tall.

favourite adjective
If something is your **favourite** thing, it is the thing you like best of all.
What is your **favourite** food?

feather noun
A bird's body is covered in **feathers** that keep it warm and dry and help it to fly.
A flamingo has pink **feathers**.

feel verb
1 If you **feel** something, you find out more about it by touching it.
She can **feel** the round shape of the coconut and its hard shell.
2 You can **feel** sad or happy, and you can feel well or sick. Feeling is what is happening to you at the time.
I **feel** sore all over.

feet see **foot**

fence noun
A **fence** is something made of wood and wire that goes round a piece of land to keep animals in or out.
Some goats got out of the field through a hole in the **fence**.

ferry noun
A **ferry** is a boat or a ship that carries people and vehicles from one place to another across a river or the sea.
He has to travel on a **ferry** every day to get to his work.

field noun
A **field** is a piece of open land with a fence or some sort of hedge round it. People keep animals or grow crops in fields.
The farmer moved his cattle to another **field**.

fill verb
If you **fill** something, you make it full.
Fill the jug with milk and put it on the table.

film noun
A **film** is a story recorded by a camera as a set of moving pictures that you watch in a cinema or on television.
*There is a good **film** on TV this evening.*

fine adjective
1 If someone feels **fine**, they feel well or okay.
*After a few days in bed, she feels **fine**.*
2 If something is **fine**, it is very thin and light.
*Down is the name we give to the **fine** feathers of some ducks and geese.*

finger noun
A **finger** is one of the four long thin parts at the end of your hands.
*Each hand has four **fingers** and one thumb.*

fire noun
1 Fire is the flames, heat and light that come from something burning.
*Hundreds of trees were burned down in the forest **fire**.*
2 A **fire** can also be a small inside fire of coal or wood in a fireplace. This kind of fire heats up a room and keeps you warm.
*There was a wood **fire** burning brightly in the fireplace.*

fire engine noun
A **fire engine** is a kind of lorry that carries firemen and their fire-fighting equipment to a fire.
*A **fire engine** went racing past us on its way to put out a fire.*

firework noun
A **firework** is a small object that sometimes goes up into the air. It explodes and gives off brightly coloured showers of light.
*There was a display of **fireworks** after the festival.*

first adjective
If someone or something is **first**, they come before anyone or anything else.
*She was the **first** person to arrive at the party.*

fish noun
A **fish** is an animal that lives in water. Fish have fins to help them swim. They breathe through gills and are covered in scales.
*Lots of people like eating cooked **fish**.*

fix verb
1 If you **fix** something, you make it work again or repair it.
*My mum **fixed** the chain on my bike so I can ride it to school again.*
2 When you **fix** something to something else, you make it stick to that thing.
*He **fixed** the TV screen to the wall.*

flag noun
A **flag** is a piece of cloth with a coloured pattern on it that can be fixed to a pole.
*All the countries of the world have their own **flag**.*

flamingo noun
A **flamingo** is a large pink bird with long legs and a curved beak.
***Flamingos** like to stand on one leg while the other leg is tucked under their body.*

floor noun
The **floor** is the flat part of a room where you walk or stand.
*The kitchen has a wooden **floor**.*

flower noun
A **flower** is the part of a plant that seeds come from. Flowers are often brightly coloured and many have a nice smell.
*I picked some **flowers** to give to my mum.*

fly¹ verb
1 If something, such as a bird, an insect or a plane, can **fly**, then it is able to move through the air, usually using wings. Helicopters fly using rotor blades.
*The bird was **flying** back to its nest with food for its chicks.*
2 If you **fly** somewhere, you travel there on a plane.
*They are going to **fly** to South Africa on holiday.*

fly² noun
A **fly** is an insect that is often black in colour and has two wings.
*The cattle were swishing their tails to get rid of the **flies**.*

food noun
Food is all the things that people and animals eat.
*We need to eat some **food** every day.*

foot noun
Your **foot** is the part of your body at the end of your leg. You stand and walk using your two feet.
*He has hurt his right **foot** and it is hard for him to walk.*

football noun
Football is a game played by two teams who try to score goals by kicking a ball into a net.
*She loves practising her **football** skills.*

forehead noun
Your **forehead** is the top part of your face above your eyes and below your hair.
*She hurt her **forehead** when she tripped and fell on the way to school.*

forest noun
A **forest** is a large piece of land covered with trees and other plants.
*There is a path through the **forest**.*

fork noun
A **fork** has three or four thin pointed bits at the end of a long handle. You use a fork to pick up food from your plate when you are eating.
*She puts knives, **forks** and spoons on the table before every meal.*

fox noun
A **fox** is a wild animal from the dog family. Foxes have bushy tails.
*Some **foxes** live and hunt for food in towns.*

free adjective
If something is **free**, it doesn't cost any money.
*There was a **free** gift with her comic.*

fresh adjective
1 If food is **fresh**, it is new or has just been made. It is not tinned or frozen.
*He had some **fresh** fruit for breakfast.*
2 If water is **fresh**, it is not salty like the water in the sea.
*Some fish live in **fresh** water and some live in seawater.*

fridge (refrigerator) noun
A **fridge** is like a large electric cupboard that keeps food cold and fresh.
*She put the milk back in the **fridge**.*

friend noun
A **friend** is someone you know very well. You like them and they like you.
*He is my best **friend**.*

frog noun
A **frog** is a small animal with webbed feet, smooth skin and big eyes. A frog can live in water and on land.
*Most **frogs** are very good at jumping thanks to their long back legs.*

frosty adjective
When the weather is **frosty**, it is very cold and a very thin layer of white ice covers the ground and plants.
*Some plants die in **frosty** weather.*

frozen adjective
If something is **frozen**, it has turned into ice or is covered by ice.
*The water in the ice-cube tray was **frozen**.*

fruit noun
Fruit is the part of a plant or tree that has seeds in it. Many fruits are sweet and nice to eat.
*I love to eat **fruit** like apples and bananas.*

full adjective
Something is **full** when it holds as much as it can possibly hold and there is no room for any more.
*The jar of sweets was **full** up to the very top.*

fun noun
Fun is when you are doing something that you enjoy and that makes you feel happy.
*We had great **fun** at my friend's birthday party.*

funny adjective
If something is **funny**, it makes us laugh.
*He made us laugh by telling **funny** jokes.*

fur noun
Fur is the thick soft hair of many animals.
*Polar bears have lots of thick soft **fur**.*

furniture noun
Furniture is the name given to all the large things in a house like tables, chairs and beds.
*When we moved house, we took all our **furniture** with us.*

Gg

game *noun*
A **game** is something with rules that you enjoy playing.
*Football is a **game** and so is cricket.*

garage *noun*
1 A **garage** is a place where some people keep their cars.
*Our **garage** is right next to our house.*
2 A **garage** can also be the place where cars are repaired.
*My mum took our car to the **garage** to get the engine fixed.*

garden *noun*
A **garden** is the land beside a house where you can grow grass, small trees, flowers and vegetables.
*We have a **garden** at the back of our house.*

gate *noun*
A **gate** is like a door in a fence or wall that allows people to come into or leave a field or a garden.
*Please shut the **gate**!*

get *verb*
1 If you **get** something, someone gives it to you.
*I hope I **get** a few presents on my birthday.*
2 If you **get** something, you buy something.
*Where did you **get** your new trainers?*

ghost *noun*
Some people believe a **ghost** is a dead person who appears in front of living people.
*He was sure he had seen a **ghost** in the old castle.*

giant *noun*
A **giant** is a very very big and strong person in stories.
*There is a **giant** in the English story 'Jack and the Beanstalk'.*

gift *noun*
A **gift** is a present that you give to someone or that someone gives to you.
*I bought a **gift** for my grandma for her 70th birthday.*

giraffe *noun*
A **giraffe** is a tall wild animal from Africa with long legs and a very long neck. Its coat is pale brown with lots of reddish-brown patches.
***Giraffes** are the tallest animals in the world.*

girl *noun*
A **girl** is a female child or a female young person.
*There are sixteen **girls** and fourteen boys in my class at school.*

give *verb*
If you **give** something to someone, you hand it over to them to keep.
*I am going to **give** my teacher a present when school closes for the summer holidays.*

glacier noun
A **glacier** is a huge amount of ice that moves very slowly down a mountain valley.
Glaciers are made over many years from ice and snow that has been tightly squeezed together.

glass noun
1 **Glass** is a hard and easily broken material that you can see through. It is used to make windows and other things like light bulbs.
The church windows were made with coloured glass.
2 A **glass** is a container for drinking that is made from glass.
She asked for a glass of water.

glasses noun
Glasses are worn in front of the eyes to help people to see better. They are made from two pieces of glass or plastic (lenses) placed in a light frame that sits on the nose and ears. The lenses make things look clearer and easier to see.
Thanks to my new glasses I can see much more clearly now.

glove noun
A **glove** is a covering for your hand that has separate spaces for each finger and your thumb.
I have red gloves that match my hat and scarf.

glue noun
Glue is a sticky mixture that is used to stick things together.
She used glue to stick her drawing in her schoolbook.

go verb
If you **go** somewhere, you move or travel from the place where you are to another place.
I go to school by bus.

goal noun
1 In games like football the **goal** is the place where the ball must go in order to score a point.
The goalkeeper couldn't stop the ball from going into the goal.
2 If you score a **goal**, you get the ball into the goal and win a point.
My dad was pleased when his team scored a goal.

goat noun
A **goat** is an animal the size of a sheep that has horns and a little beard.
Goats give us milk that can be made into goat's cheese.

gold noun
Gold is a yellow shiny metal that is worth a lot of money.
Gold can be made into beautiful jewellery.

goldfish noun
Goldfish are small reddish-gold fish that live in fresh water.
In some countries, goldfish are kept as pets.

good adjective
1 If a person is **good**, they are behaving well.
*When we are **good**, our mum and dad are very happy!*
2 If something is **good**, it is very enjoyable or interesting.
*I thought it was a **good** book.*

goodbye
Goodbye is what we say when we are leaving someone or they are leaving us. We also say goodbye when we have finished talking to someone on the phone.
*I said '**Goodbye**!' to my friend as the train began to slowly move away.*

goose noun
A **goose** is a large water bird with strong short legs, webbed feet and a long neck.
*In some countries, tame **geese** are used as guard animals because they make a lot of noise when they see a stranger.*

grandchild noun
Someone's **grandchild** is the child of their son or their daughter.
*My grandma says I'm her favourite **grandchild**, but I think she says that to all her grandchildren.*

granddaughter noun
Someone's **granddaughter** is the daughter of their daughter or their son.
*My grandmother and grandfather have two **granddaughters** – my sister and me!*

grandfather (grandpa, granddad) noun
Someone's **grandfather** is the father of their mother or their father.
*I have two **grandfathers** – my mum's father and my dad's father.*

grandmother (gran, granny, grandma) noun
Someone's **grandmother** is the mother of their mother or their father.
*Her **grandmother** looks after her when her mum and dad are at work.*

grandparents noun
Someone's **grandparents** are the parents of their mother or their father.
*My **grandparents** came to visit us last week.*

grandson noun
Someone's **grandson** is the son of their daughter or their son.
*The little girl's grandma and grandpa have one **grandson** – her brother!*

grape noun
A **grape** is a small green or purple fruit like a berry. Grapes grow in bunches with other grapes on a grape vine.
***Grapes** are used for making wine.*

grass noun
Grass is a green plant with very thin leaves that grows close to the ground.
*Animals like cattle and sheep like to eat **grass**.*

grasshopper noun
A **grasshopper** is an insect that eats plants. It has long back legs that are good for jumping. Grasshoppers rub their legs against their wings to make a chirping sound.
Grasshoppers live on the ground and jump to get away from danger.

great adjective
1 If something is **great**, it is large in number or size.
There was a great big hole in the road.
2 If someone is **great**, they are important, famous or powerful.
Nelson Mandela was a great man.
3 If you say something is **great**, you mean that it is very good.
We had a great time at the party.

green adjective
If something is **green**, it is the colour of grass in summer.
The leaves on a banana plant are green.

grey adjective
If something is **grey**, it is the colour of the sky on a rainy day.
He has to wear grey trousers as part of his school uniform.

guinea pig noun
A **guinea pig** is a small furry animal that has no tail and is kept as a pet.
Guinea pigs live for four to five years.

guitar noun
A **guitar** is a musical instrument with a long neck and six strings. You hold a guitar on your knee or with a strap over your shoulder. You play it using your fingers.
He is learning to play the guitar.

Hh

hair noun
1 **Hair** is the soft covering, made up of very fine thread-like strands, that grows on the skin of people and animals.
When I get a big fright, the hairs on the back of my neck stand up.
2 Your **hair** is made up of all the hairs growing on your head.
I like to wash my hair every day.

half noun
A **half** is one of the two equal parts that make up a whole.
I divided the chocolate bar into two equal halves – one half for me and the other half for my brother!

hammer noun
A **hammer** is a tool with a long handle and a heavy metal head that is used to hit nails into something.
I used a hammer to put a nail in the wall.

hamster noun
A **hamster** is a small furry animal that is a very popular pet in some countries.
Pet hamsters like to live on their own.

hand noun
Your **hand** is the part of your body at the end of your arm. Each of your two hands has four fingers and a thumb. We use our hands to hold things.
My hands were very dirty so I washed them before eating my lunch.

handbag noun
A **handbag** is a small bag used by women to carry things like money, keys and make-up.
My mum has a new red handbag.

a b c d e f g **h** i j k l m n o p q r s t u v w x y z

handle noun
A **handle** is the part of something that is used to hold it.
*Cups and mugs have **handles**.*

happy adjective
If you are **happy**, you feel cheerful and in a good mood.
*I was very **happy** on my birthday.*

hard adjective
1 If something is **hard**, it is firm or solid, not soft, and it is difficult to break.
*Iron is a very **hard** metal.*
2 If something is **hard**, it is difficult and not easy to do.
*It is **hard** to ride a bike for the first time.*

hat noun
A **hat** is a covering for your head.
*When she was outside in the sun, she wore a **hat**.*

hate verb
1 If you **hate** someone or something, you do not like them at all.
*She **hates** broccoli.*
2 If you **hate** doing something, you are not happy when you are doing it.
*I **hate** walking to school in the rain.*

have verb
1 If you **have** something, you own it and it belongs to you.
*I **have** four pairs of shoes.*
2 When you **have** something, it is happening to you at that time.
*I **have** a very bad cold and I can't go to school today.*

head noun
Your **head** is the top part of your body that contains your brain, your eyes, nose, mouth and ears.
*He fell downstairs and bumped his **head**.*

headphones noun
Headphones are a pair of earphones joined by a band that you wear over your ears so that you can to listen to music or the radio on your own.

*My big sister wears **headphones** so that she can listen to music on her mobile phone.*

heart noun
Your **heart** is the organ inside your chest that pumps blood round your body.
*After I ran all the way home, my **heart** was beating very fast.*

heat¹ verb
If you **heat** something, you make it warm or hot.
*We use a wood fire to **heat** our house.*

heat² noun
Heat is the hotness of something. Heat is the opposite of cold
*The sun's light and **heat** take about eight minutes to travel from the sun to the earth.*

heater noun
A **heater** is a device that makes you feel warm.
*The room was cold so we switched on the electric **heater**.*

hedge noun
A **hedge** is a row of bushes or small trees that grow close together and act as a fence.
*Some types of birds make their nests in **hedges**.*

hedgehog noun
A **hedgehog** is a small animal with a coat of hard, pointed spiny hairs.
*A **hedgehog** sleeps during the day and hunts for food at night.*

helicopter noun
A **helicopter** is a small aircraft that uses a set of long blades to make it move straight up and down or along.
*The rescue **helicopter** lifted the man with a broken leg off the mountain and took him to hospital.*

helmet noun
A **helmet** is a kind of hard hat that you wear to protect your head.
*In a lot of countries, the law says you must wear a **helmet** when you ride a motorbike.*

help verb
If you **help** someone, you do something that makes it easier for them to do whatever they are doing.
*I **helped** the old lady to cross the busy road.*

hen noun
A **hen** is a female chicken. People eat the eggs laid by hens.
*Some people keep a few **hens** in their back garden.*

herd noun
A **herd** is a large group of animals that live together.
*A **herd** of elephants walked slowly down to the river.*

hide verb
If you **hide** something, you put it in a place where no one can see it or find it.
*The old lady **hides** her money in a tin under her bed.*

high adjective
If something is **high**, it goes up a long way.
*It was a very **high** building.*

hill noun
A **hill** is a piece of high ground that is smaller than a mountain.
*It didn't take us too long to climb to the top of the **hill**.*

hippo (hippopotamus) noun
A **hippo** is a very large African animal with a heavy body and short legs. It spends most of its time in water but comes out at night to eat grass.
***Hippos** live for forty to fifty years.*

hit verb
If you **hit** something or someone, you beat or strike them hard with a tool, or your hand, or a weapon of some kind.
*I **hit** the nail with a hammer.*

hole noun
A **hole** is a hollow place or an empty space in something.
*He has a **hole** in his T-shirt.*

holiday noun
A **holiday** is a time when you are away from school or work.
*We are looking forward to the school **holidays**.*

home noun
Your **home** is the place where you live.
*We all love our new **home**.*

homework noun
Homework is schoolwork that has to be done at home.
*I had lots of **homework** yesterday.*

honey noun
Honey is the sweet and thick sticky liquid made by bees from nectar.
*She loves **honey** on her toast.*

hop verb
1 If you **hop**, you jump about on one foot.
*He **hopped** about in pain after dropping a hammer on his toe.*
2 If a bird or an animal **hops**, it moves along with small jumps.
*The little bird **hopped** along the path.*

horrible adjective
1 If something is **horrible**, it is shocking or dreadful.
*There has been a **horrible** accident on the road near our school.*
2 If someone or something is **horrible**, they are bad and not very nice.
*The food from the takeaway was **horrible**.*

horse noun
A **horse** is a four-legged animal with a long mane and tail that is used for riding, racing or pulling things along.
*He rides his **horse** every day.*

hospital noun
A **hospital** is a building where people that are ill or injured are looked after by doctors and nurses.
*She went to **hospital** when she was very ill with malaria.*

hot adjective
If someone or something is **hot**, they are very warm. Hot is the opposite of cold.
*She had a cup of **hot** tea.*

hotel noun
A **hotel** is a building where people pay to eat and sleep when they are away from home.
*There is a big **hotel** near the airport.*

house noun
Your **house** is the building in which you live.
*He lives in a **house** near the sea.*

hug verb
If you **hug** someone, you put your arms round them and hold them very close to you.
*She **hugged** her sister.*

huge adjective
If something is **huge**, it is very very big.
*There was a **huge** storm with lots of heavy rain.*

hungry adjective
If you are **hungry**, your tummy feels empty and you want something to eat.
*They were very **hungry** after their long walk.*

hurt verb
If you **hurt** yourself, you do something that gives you pain in a part of your body.
*My grandma fell and **hurt** her knee.*

hut noun
A **hut** is a small house or shelter that can be made of different kinds of materials such as wood, stone, animal skins or mud.
*There was a row of **huts** next to the river.*

Ii

ice noun
Ice is frozen water. It is hard and cold and slippery.
*She wanted some **ice** in her glass of water.*

iceberg noun
An **iceberg** is a very large piece of ice that breaks away from a glacier or an ice sheet and floats out to sea.
*Most of the **ice** in an iceberg is under the water.*

ice cream noun
Ice cream is a sweet, creamy mixture that has been frozen.
*She loves chocolate **ice cream**.*

icicle noun
An **icicle** is a long thin stick of ice. It is made from dripping water that has frozen.
*There were **icicles** hanging from the roof.*

idea noun
An **idea** is a kind of plan for doing something that you have been thinking about.
*The teacher had some good **ideas** for a class outing.*

igloo noun
An **igloo** is a small house made from blocks of snow.
*The Eskimo peoples of the Arctic have used **igloos** as winter homes for hundreds of years.*

ill adjective
When you are **ill**, you are not well but sick with an illness or a disease.
*I came home from school early because I was **ill**.*

illustration noun
An **illustration** is a picture in a book, magazine or newspaper.
*There are some beautiful **illustrations** in the old storybook.*

important adjective
1 If something is **important**, it has great value and matters a lot.
*In places where there is a lot of malaria, it is **important** to sleep under a mosquito net.*
2 If someone is **important**, they often have lots of power and lots of money. Many important people have done something special that has made them famous.
*Kings, queens, presidents and prime ministers are all **important** people.*

insect noun
An **insect** is a very small creature with six legs and a body divided into three parts. Some **insects** have wings.
*A bee is an **insect**.*

inside adverb
If someone or something is **inside**, they are indoors not outside in the fresh air.
*The children played **inside** because it was raining.*

instrument noun
1 An **instrument** is a tool that people use to make difficult jobs easier to do.
*The nurse laid out the **instruments** to be used during the operation.*
2 An **instrument** is something that you use to make musical sounds.
*The sitar is an Indian musical **instrument**.*

interest noun
If you show **interest** in something, you like it and want to know more about it.
*He has shown a great **interest** in music since he was a little boy.*

interesting adjective
If you think something is **interesting**, it means you like it and you want to know more about it.
*I think the film about tigers was very **interesting**.*

internet noun
The **internet** is a huge computer system called a network.
*Any computer can connect with any other computer as long as they are both part of the **internet**.*

invitation noun
If you get an **invitation** to an event, someone is asking you to come to that event.
*We got an **invitation** to our cousin's wedding.*

invite verb
If you **invite** someone, you ask them if they can go somewhere or do something with you.
*My aunt has **invited** us all to lunch tomorrow.*

iron noun
1 An **iron** is an electrical device with a handle and a flat metal bottom. When an iron is heated, it is used to smooth the wrinkles out of clothes.
*I pressed the wrinkles out of my shirt with our new **iron**.*

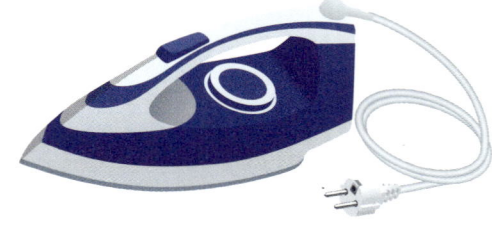

2 Iron is also the name for a strong, hard, grey metal.
*The old gate is made of **iron**.*

island noun
An **island** is a piece of land with water all around it.
*He went out to the **island** on a boat.*

itchy adjective
When your skin is **itchy**, it feels like you want to rub it gently with your nails.
*The insect bite made her skin feel **itchy**.*

Jj

jacket *noun*
A **jacket** is like a short coat. It can be worn with trousers, a skirt or a dress.
*I left my **jacket** on the bus.*

jam *noun*
Jam is a sweet food made by cooking fruit with a lot of sugar.
*I love apricot **jam** on my toast.*

jar *noun*
A **jar** is a small glass container with a wide opening and a lid.
*We made enough apricot jam to fill four jam **jars**!*

jeans *noun*
Jeans are trousers made out of a strong blue cloth called denim.
*She likes to wear **jeans** or shorts.*

jelly *noun*
Jelly is a kind of soft sweet food made with fruit flavours, sugar and gelatine. Jelly wobbles when it is moved.
*We put the strawberry **jelly** in the fridge to set.*

jellyfish *noun*
A **jellyfish** is an animal that lives in the sea. It has a soft jelly-like body that looks like an umbrella and long thin parts that can sting you (tentacles).
***Jellyfish** are found in every ocean in the world.*

jersey *noun*
A **jersey** is a piece of clothing for the upper part of your body. It has sleeves and an opening for your head. It does not open down the front.
*My grandma is busy knitting a **jersey** for my brother.*

jewellery *noun*
Jewellery is small and pretty things made from jewels and metals like gold and silver.
*My sister has some **jewellery**.*

jigsaw (jigsaw puzzle) *noun*
A **jigsaw** is a picture puzzle consisting of a picture that has been broken up into small pieces. You have to place each of these pieces in the correct place until the picture is back together again.
*The **jigsaw** had 500 pieces.*

job *noun*
1 A **job** is any work that is done for money.
His dad has a job as a car mechanic.
2 A **job** can also be a piece of work.
*We have a few **jobs** to do around the house to make it clean and tidy.*

joke *noun*
A **joke** is something a person says or does to make people laugh.
*I heard a funny **joke** yesterday.*

jug noun
A **jug** is a container with a handle and a spout. It is used for holding liquids.
*She fetched a **jug** of milk from the fridge.*

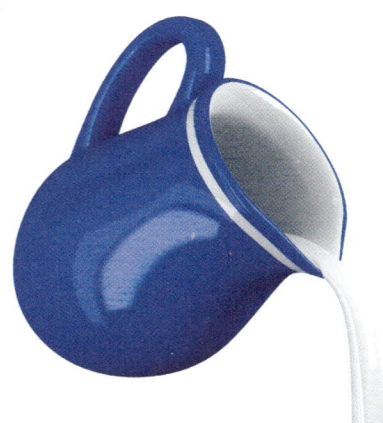

juice noun
Juice is the liquid that is in some fruit and vegetables.
*They had a drink of orange **juice**.*

jump verb
If you **jump**, you move your body quickly and suddenly off the ground and into the air or over something.
*She **jumped** with fright when she saw the snake.*

jumper noun
Jumper is another word for a jersey.
*She took off her red **jumper** because she was feeling very hot.*

jungle noun
A **jungle** is a piece of wild land in a hot country. It is covered with lots of tall trees and plants growing very close together.
*They could hear the gorillas moving through the **jungle**.*

kangaroo noun
A **kangaroo** is a large Australian animal with a long tail and powerful hind legs for jumping and hopping.
*A baby **kangaroo** is called a 'joey'.*

key noun
A **key** is a small piece of metal that fits into the lock on a door and is used to lock or unlock the door.
*My brother lost the front door **key** and we couldn't get into our house!*

kick verb
If you **kick** something, you hit it hard with your foot.
*He **kicked** the ball into the goal.*

king noun
A **king** is the most important man in a country's royal family. Sometimes that means he is also the ruler of that country.
*He was the **king** for twenty years.*

kiss verb
When you **kiss** someone, you touch them with your lips. You kiss people when you are saying hello or goodbye or when you want to show them that you like them.
*His mum always **kisses** him on the cheek before she leaves for work.*

kitchen *noun*
A **kitchen** is the room in a house where all the cooking is done.
*We have a gas cooker in our **kitchen**.*

kite *noun*
A **kite** is a light frame (of different shapes) covered with paper, thin cloth or plastic. The frame has a long piece of string fixed to it so that you can hold on to it as it flies up into the air on a windy day.
*My **kite** keeps flying higher and higher in the wind.*

kitten *noun*
A **kitten** is a baby cat or a very young cat.
*Our cat has four **kittens**.*

knee *noun*
Your **knee** is the middle part of your leg where it bends.
*My grandma gets sore **knees** when she has to walk for a long time.*

knife *noun*
A **knife** is a thin flat piece of metal with a handle that is used for cutting up food.
*She cut up the meat with a sharp **knife**.*

knight *noun*
In the past, a **knight** was a man who wore heavy armour. Knights were expected to be very good at riding horses and fighting.
***Knights** used to fight on horseback for their king or lord.*

koala *noun*
A **koala** is an Australian animal that looks like a small bear with grey fur.
***Koalas** eat the leaves of the eucalyptus tree.*

knock *verb*
1 If you **knock** on a door, you hit it hard a few times to make a noise that the person inside can hear.
*I heard him **knocking** on the door and went to let him in.*
2 If you **knock** something or someone over, you run into them or hit them and make them fall.
*'Who **knocked** over that glass of milk?'*

knot *noun*
A **knot** is a way of fixing two pieces of string, or ribbon, or rope together. A knot is also a loop or a twist in a piece of rope, string or ribbon.
*'I can't undo this **knot** – it is too tight.'*

Ll

label *noun*
A **label** is a small piece of paper or cloth that is fixed to an object. It has writing or printing on it to tell you something about the object.
*The **label** on the dress said it was made of cotton.*

ladder *noun*
A **ladder** is a set of short bars that form steps between two long bars. A ladder is used to reach high places and it can be moved around.
*He had to use a **ladder** to reach the roof.*

ladle *noun*
A **ladle** is a kind of large spoon with a deep round part and a long handle that is used to serve food like soup.
*I had a **ladle** of chicken soup for lunch.*

lady *noun*
Lady is a name given to a woman who knows how to behave well among other people and is kind to other people.
*The old woman was poor but she always behaved like a **lady**.*

ladybird *noun*
A **ladybird** is a small round beetle that is red or yellow with black spots.
***Ladybirds** are useful in gardens because they eat the insects that eat plants.*

lake *noun*
A **lake** is a large area of water that has land all around it.
*Fishermen catch fish on the **lake** near our home.*

lamb *noun*
A **lamb** is a young sheep.
*Sheep and their **lambs** are mainly found in Australia, New Zealand, southern and central South American countries, and in Britain.*

last *adjective*
If someone or something is **last**, they come after all the others.
*My brother was the **last** pupil to go inside after breaktime.*

late *adverb*
If someone or something is **late**, they arrive after the usual or right time.
*Because her train was **late**, she was late arriving at school.*

laugh *verb*
If you **laugh**, you smile and make the sound that people make when they think something is very funny.
*The TV show was so funny that it made us all **laugh**.*

lawn *noun*
A **lawn** is the green part of a garden that is covered in short grass.
*He used a lawnmower to cut the grass on the **lawn**.*

leaf noun
A **leaf** is the thin, green part of a plant that is at the end of the plant's stem or stalk.
*The tree was covered in new green **leaves**.*

left adjective
Left is used to describe something that is on the same side of your body as your heart.
*Her **left** ear is very sore.*

leg noun
Your **leg** is one of the two long parts of your body that you stand on and use for walking.
*He broke his **leg** playing football.*

leggings noun
Leggings are like thin tight trousers. Girls and women wear leggings under tops or dresses.
*My sister is wearing a pair of black **leggings** under her dress.*

lemon noun
A **lemon** is a fruit with a thick yellow skin and sour juice.
*When I have a sore throat, I like to drink hot water with **lemon** juice and honey.*

leopard noun
A **leopard** is a large wild animal from the cat family whose fur is either black or a yellowish colour with dark spots.
***Leopards** live in the forests of Africa and Asia.*

letter noun
1 A **letter** is how we write a sound in a language. When letters are put together they make words.
*In English the **letters** 'c', 'a', and 't' make the word 'cat'.*
2 A **letter** is also a message from one person to another that is written down on paper, put in an envelope and posted.

*I wrote a **letter** to my aunt to say thank you for the money she sent me.*

lick verb
If someone or something **licks** something, they move their tongue over it to find out what it tastes like, or to make it wet, or to clean it.
*A cat **licks** its fur to make it clean.*

lid noun
A **lid** is the top part of a jar, a bottle or a box that can be taken off.
*'Please put the **lid** back on the jar of peanut butter.'*

light¹ noun
A **light** is something like an electric bulb or a torch whose brightness lets you see things when it is dark.
*'It is getting quite dark in here. Please switch on the **light**.'*

light² adjective
If something is **light**, it is not heavy and weighs very little.
*I packed very few clothes so my case is quite **light**.*

lightning noun
Lightning is a sudden bright flash in the sky during a thunderstorm.
*My dog gets very frightened when there is thunder and **lightning**.*

like verb
1 When you **like** someone, you think they are nice and you enjoy their company.
*I **like** my aunt very much.*
2 When you **like** doing something, you enjoy doing it.
*He **likes** playing football.*

lion noun
A **lion** is a large wild animal from the cat family with yellowish-brown fur. The male lion has lots of long fur round his neck.
***Lions** live in Africa and southern Asia.*

lip noun
Your **lip** is one the two soft parts of your face that form the edges of your mouth.
*Her lower **lip** was bleeding after she tripped and fell.*

liquid noun
Liquids, such as water, can move freely or flow from one container into another.
*When you freeze a **liquid** it becomes a solid. For example, water turns to ice when it is frozen.*

litter noun
Litter is the rubbish, like empty plastic bottles and crisp packets, that people drop in the street or in other public places.
*There was a lot of **litter** on the beach and in the sea.*

little adjective
If someone or something is **little**, they are small not big.
*His dog was a **little** dog but it had a long tail!*

live verb
If you **live** in a place, that is where your home is.
*We have **lived** in this house for over ten years.*

living room noun
The **living room** is the room in a house where people spend a lot of time together.
*The whole family was in the **living room** to watch the football match on TV.*

lizard noun
A **lizard** is a reptile with a long body, four short legs and a long tail.
*The skin of a **lizard** is covered in scales.*

loaf noun
A **loaf** is bread that has been baked in one piece. A loaf can be many different shapes.
*She cut the **loaf** of bread into slices.*

log noun
A **log** is a large piece of wood from a tree that has fallen down or been cut down.
*Some **logs** are cut up and used as firewood.*

lolly noun
A **lolly** is a large sweet on a stick. An ice lolly is a piece of frozen juice or ice cream on a stick.
*We all had an ice **lolly** to cool us down.*

long adjective
1 If something is **long**, it measures a lot from one end to the other end.
*My classroom is at the end of a **long** corridor.*
2 If something is **long**, it can also mean that it lasts for a large amount of time.
*She had a **long** wait for the next bus.*

look verb
If you **look** at something, you move your eyes so that you can see it.
*'**Look** outside – it is raining!'*

lorry noun
A **lorry** is a large vehicle that carries things by road from one place to another place.
*The **lorry** broke down on the motorway.*

loud adjective
If something is **loud**, it is making a lot of noise.
*'I can't hear what you are saying because of the **loud** music.'*

love verb
1 If you **love** someone, you are very fond of them and care very much for them.
*She **loves** her new baby brother.*
2 If you **love** something, you are very interested in it and enjoy it.
*He **loves** dancing.*

lovely adjective
1 If something or someone is **lovely**, they are beautiful.
*She was wearing a **lovely** dress.*
2 When something is **lovely**, it can also mean it is very enjoyable.
*We had a **lovely** time in the nature reserve.*
3 If someone is **lovely**, they are kind and friendly.
*My sister is a **lovely** person.*

low adjective
If something is **low**, it is not high.
***Low** clouds covered the hills.*

lunch noun
Lunch is the light meal we eat in the middle of the day.
*I like to have a sandwich for **lunch**.*

Mm

machine noun
A **machine** is a device that does a job, often using electricity.
*I am learning how to use a sewing **machine** at school.*

magic noun
Magic is when something impossible seems to happen. Magicians do magic tricks and seem to have special powers.
*As if by **magic**, the magician put a white rabbit in his top hat and made it disappear.*

magician noun
1 In stories, a **magician** is a person with magical powers.
*The **magician** cast a spell to make objects come to life.*
2 In real life, **magicians** use all sorts of tricks to make people think they have magical powers.
*The **magician** made a white rabbit appear out of his top hat.*

magnet noun
A **magnet** is a piece of iron or steel that can pull other pieces of iron or steel towards it.

*There are lots of fridge **magnets** attached to her fridge door.*

make verb
1 When you **make** something, you build it or put it all together.
*My big sister **makes** all her own clothes.*
2 When someone **makes** you do something, you have to do it even if you don't want to.
*At dinner, my dad **makes** me eat cabbage.*

make-up noun
If you use **make-up**, you use products like lipstick, foundation, blusher or powder on your face to make you look better.
*She puts on her **make-up** every morning before she goes to work.*

mammal noun
A **mammal** is an animal that breathes air, has a backbone and skin with hair. A young mammal is fed with milk produced by its mother.
*Cows, dogs, bears and human beings are **mammals**.*

man noun
A **man** is an adult male person.
*Her uncle was a very tall **man**.*

map noun
A **map** is a kind of drawing that shows all the details of a piece of land or a country (including roads, towns and rivers), as if you were looking at them from above.
*We can see where the road goes on the **map**.*

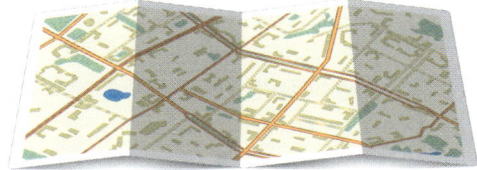

mat noun
A **mat** is a kind of small carpet for covering part of a floor.
*There is a small soft **mat** next to my bed.*

material noun
Material is cloth or fabric of some kind.
*We went to the market to find some **material** to make some new cushion covers.*

mean verb
If someone asks what a word **means**, they want you to explain what that word is about or what it is saying.
*She asked me 'What does sad **mean**?'*
*I replied 'Sad **means** being unhappy about something.'*

meat noun
Meat is the flesh and organs of animals like cattle and sheep. Some people cook and eat meat.
*Vegetarians don't eat **meat**.*

mess noun
A **mess** happens when things are left lying around and not put away or cleaned.
*My room was a **mess** until I picked everything up and put things back where they belong.*

milk noun
1 Milk is the white liquid produced by female mammals to feed their babies.
*The sheep had plenty of **milk** to feed both her lambs.*
2 People use **milk** from cows, goats and sheep as a drink and to make food like butter and cheese.
*She drinks a glass of **milk** with her breakfast.*

mirror noun
A **mirror** is a piece of glass with a silvery layer on the back in which you can see yourself.
*My big sister puts on her make-up in front of a **mirror**.*

mistake noun
1 If you make a **mistake**, you do something wrong but without meaning to do it wrong.
*She made a **mistake** by getting onto the wrong bus.*
2 A **mistake** is something that is not right or correct.
*There were a lot of **mistakes** in his maths homework.*

money noun
Money is the coins and banknotes you use to buy things.
*My brother used some of his **money** to buy new trainers.*

monkey noun
A **monkey** is an animal with soft fur, strong arms and a long tail. Most monkeys live in or around trees in hot countries.
*A group of **monkeys** is called a tribe or a troop of monkeys.*

monster noun
A **monster** in stories or films is a very large ugly creature that frightens people.
*In her dream she was being chased by a horrible **monster**.*

month noun
A year is made up of twelve **months**: January, February, March, April, May, June, July, August, September, October, November, December.
*Her birthday is in the **month** of July.*

moon noun
The **moon** is a large round object that shines in the sky at night as it moves round the earth.
*Twelve astronauts walked on the **moon** between 1969 and 1972.*

mop noun
A **mop** is a bunch of thick strings or a sponge with a long handle that is used to wash the floor.
*I used a **mop** to wash the kitchen floor.*

morning noun
Morning is the time of day between the sun coming up and 12 o'clock in the middle of the day.
*It rained all **morning** but the sun came out in the afternoon.*

mother noun
A **mother** is a woman who has given birth to a child or has adopted a child.
*The little girl's **mother** took her to see the doctor.*

motor noun
A **motor** is an engine that gives power to a vehicle or a boat.
*He started the **motor** and the boat slowly moved away.*

motorbike noun
A **motorbike** is a two-wheeled vehicle with a motor.
*He took his friend for a ride on his **motorbike**.*

motorway noun
A **motorway** is a wide road for vehicles that are travelling fast.
*We went to the airport on the **motorway**.*

mountain noun
A **mountain** is a very high hill.
*They were very tired by the time they reached the top of the **mountain**.*

mouse noun
1 A **mouse** is a small furry animal with sharp front teeth and a long tail.
A mouse doesn't see very well but it has very good hearing.

2 A computer **mouse** is a small device that moves the small flashing line (cursor) on a computer screen.
*She held the **mouse** in her hand and used it to move the cursor back to the top of her computer screen.*

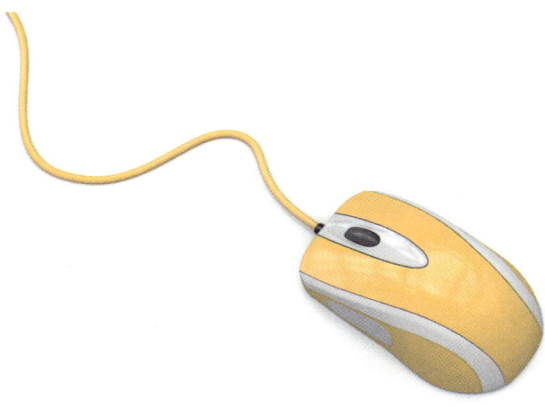

mud noun
Mud is wet sticky earth that goes hard when it dries.
*The car got stuck in the **mud**.*

mug noun
A **mug** is a large cup with straight sides and a handle that is not used with a saucer.
*My dad likes a **mug** of coffee with his breakfast.*

museum noun
A **museum** is a place where there are lots of old things that people can come and look at.
*She loves history and likes to visit **museums**.*

mushroom noun
A **mushroom** is a kind of plant with a round top and a short stem. Some wild mushrooms are poisonous.
*We saw lots of **mushrooms** when we went for a walk in the forest.*

music noun
Music is the pleasant sound made by people singing and playing instruments.
*She loves listening to **music** on the radio.*

mystery noun
A **mystery** is something that is not understood, known or explained.
*The cat has disappeared and I don't know where it has gone. It is a **mystery**.*

mutton noun
Mutton is meat from an older sheep. Meat from a young sheep is called lamb.
*We have **mutton** and rice to eat today.*

myth noun
A **myth** is a story from an ancient time.
*My favourite **myths** are stories about animals.*

Nn

nail noun
1 A **nail** is a thin pointed piece of metal with a flat head. You hit a nail into wood with a hammer.
*He used **nails** to join the two pieces of wood together.*

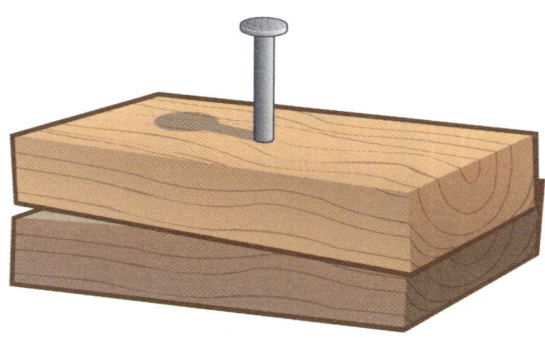

2 A **nail (fingernail)** is also the name for the thin hard covering at the end of your fingers and toes.
*She painted her **nails** with a bright red nail polish.*

name noun
A **name** is what someone or something is called.
*Their new puppy's **name** is Bella.*

naughty adjective
If someone is **naughty**, they are behaving badly.
*The **naughty** children did not listen to their teacher.*

neck noun
Your **neck** is the part of your body between your head and the rest of your body.
*She was wearing a scarf round her **neck**.*

necklace noun
A **necklace** is a piece of jewellery that you wear around your neck.
*My grandma always wears a silver **necklace**.*

needle noun
A **needle** is a small thin piece of shiny metal with a point at one end and a hole (called the eye) at the other end. A needle is used with thread when sewing.
*I pushed the cotton thread through the eye of the **needle**.*

nest noun
A **nest** is a home that is made by birds and some animals for their young.
*Birds lay their eggs and raise their chicks in **nests**.*

net noun
A **net** is made from lengths of string, wire or plastic, fixed together in such a way that there are lots of small open spaces for air or water to go through.
*Some fishermen catch **fish** using nets.*

new adjective
If something is **new**, it has only just been made and no one has used it before.
*Her mum is going to buy her a **new** T-shirt.*

newspaper see **paper** 2

nice adjective

1 If something is **nice**, you like it and find it enjoyable.
*The children had a **nice** time playing with their friends.*

2 If someone is **nice**, you think they are friendly and kind.
*She is a very **nice** person.*

night noun

Night is the time of day between sunset and sunrise when it is dark.
*Most of us sleep at **night**.*

no¹

1 You say **no** when someone asks if you have done something and you have not done it.
'Have you read this book?'
*'**No**, I haven't.'*

2 You say **no** in answer to a question if you don't agree with the person asking the question.
'I think it is going to rain. Do you?'
*'**No**, I don't think it is going to rain.'*

3 You say **no** in answer to a question if you don't want to do what the person asking the question wants to do.
'Do you want to play a new game?'
*'**No**, thanks.'*

4 You say **no** in answer to a question if you don't want what the person asking the question is offering you.
'Do you want a chocolate?'
*'**No**, thank you.'*

no²

If you say there is **no** something, you are saying there is not any of it, not even one of it.
*There are **no** biscuits left in the tin.*

nose noun

Your **nose** is the part of your face below your eyes and above your mouth that you use for breathing or smelling things.
*His **nose** was blocked and he couldn't smell anything.*

now adverb

If something is happening **now**, it is happening at this moment.
*It was pouring with rain this morning but **now** the sun is shining.*

number noun

A **number** is a word used in counting and measuring.
*One (1), twenty (20) and one hundred (100) are **numbers**.*

nurse noun

A **nurse** is someone who looks after people when they are sick in hospital.
*The **nurse** was busy all day from seven in the morning to seven at night.*

nursery school noun

A **nursery school** is a school for young children between the ages of three and five.
*My little sister goes to **nursery school** every day.*

nut noun

A **nut** is the fruit of some trees.
*A walnut is a **nut** with a hard shell and a softer part inside that you can eat.*

Oo

ocean noun
An **ocean** is a very large area of salt water or sea.
The world's five oceans are the Arctic, Atlantic, Indian, Pacific and Southern Oceans.

octopus noun
An **octopus** is a sea creature with a soft body and eight long arms called tentacles.
An octopus has a mouth with a strong beak that helps it crack the shells of crabs.

odd adjective
1 If something is **odd**, it is strange or unusual.
He was wearing a very odd hat.
2 **Odd** numbers are numbers that cannot be divided exactly by two.
One, three, five, seven and nine are odd numbers.

off adverb
1 If you go **off** somewhere, you go away from that place.
The girl ran off without saying goodbye.
2 If something that uses electricity is **off**, it is no longer using electricity and will not work.
The TV is off.

old adjective
1 If someone is **old**, they are no longer young and have lived for a long time.
My grandma is old but she is still lots of fun!
2 If something is **old**, it has been around for a long time and is no longer new.
We spent the morning in the old part of the town.

olive noun
An **olive** is the small green or black fruit of the olive tree. Olives have a hard stone in the middle and are used as a food and for making olive oil.
My mum likes olives on her pizza.

on adverb
If something that uses electricity is **on**, it is using electricity and will work.
The TV is on.

onion noun
An **onion** is a small round vegetable that grows under the ground. It has lots of layers and a strong smell and taste.
My dad loves cheese and onion in his sandwich.

open¹ *adjective*
If a door is **open**, it is not closed.
*He came into the room through the **open** door.*

open² *verb*
When you **open** something, it is no longer shut or closed.
*'I have a surprise,' he said as he **opened** the box and took out a new pair of trainers.*

opposite¹ *adjective*
1 If something is **opposite**, it is facing you or directly across from you.
*My friend and I live on **opposite** sides of the street.*
2 If something is **opposite**, it is completely different.
*He is too thin but his friend has the **opposite** problem – he is too fat.*

opposite² *noun*
An **opposite** is a person, thing or idea that is completely different from another.
*The words 'short' and 'tall' are **opposites**.*

orange¹ *noun*
An **orange** is a round juicy fruit with a thick orange skin. Oranges are peeled and eaten fresh, or squeezed for their juice, or made into an orange jam called marmalade.
*Most **oranges** are grown for their juice.*

orange² *adjective*
If something is **orange**, it is the colour of the skin of an orange.
*The sky was a lovely **orange** colour at sunset.*

outing *noun*
An **outing** is a day trip somewhere that people go on for fun.
*On Saturday we went on an **outing** to the zoo.*

outside¹ *adverb*
When someone is **outside**, they are outdoors in the open air and not inside a building.
*We love to play **outside** on sunny days.*

outside² *adjective*
If something is **outside**, it is not inside a building.
*The **outside** walls of my house are painted white.*

owl *noun*
An **owl** is a bird with soft feathers, large eyes, a hooked beak and a loud hooting call.
*Most **owls** hunt at night.*

Pp

paddle verb
When people **paddle** in water, they walk around in their bare feet in water that is not very deep.
*The children **paddled** in the shallow water at the edge of the sea.*

page noun
A **page** is one side of a sheet of paper in a book or a notebook.
*'For reading homework, please read from the start of **page** 9 to the end of page 12,' said their teacher.*

paint noun
1 **Paint** is a coloured liquid that is used to protect the walls on the inside and the outside of a house and to make them look nice.
*I chose some blue **paint** for my bedroom walls.*
2 Different kinds of paint are used to paint pictures, including oil, acrylic and watercolour.
*She uses oil paint to **paint** her pictures.*

painting noun
A **painting** is a picture that has been made by someone using paint on paper or canvas (a kind of strong cloth).
*We went to an art gallery in the city to see the **paintings** of famous artists.*

pair noun
A **pair** of things is a set of two objects that are like each other and are used together.
*He is going to buy a new **pair** of shoes.*

pan (saucepan) noun
A **pan** is a round metal container with a handle and a lid that is used for cooking food.
*I put the rice into a **pan** of hot water.*

panda noun
A **panda** is a large bear with black and white fur. Pandas eat bamboo.
***Pandas** come from China.*

papaya see pawpaw

paper noun
1 **Paper** is a material made of lots of tiny bits of soft, wet wood (called wood pulp) and other fibres. This pulp is pressed into thin flat sheets of paper like the ones we write and draw on.
*She drew a lovely picture on a sheet of **paper**.*
2 A **paper** is another word for a **newspaper**. A paper has large folded sheets of printed paper that contain news and other information for people to read.
***Papers** are sold every day of the week.*

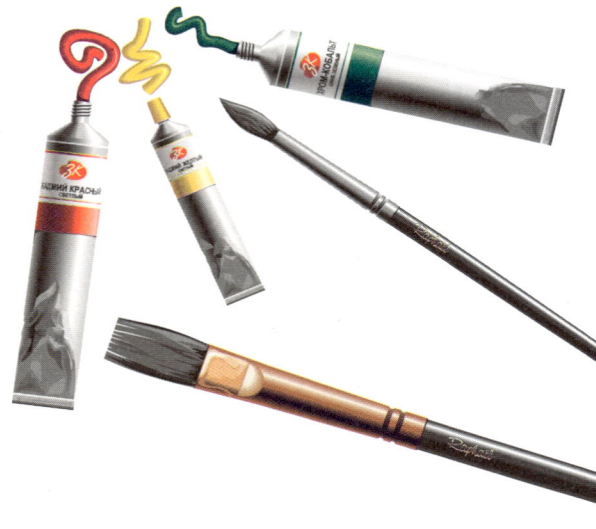

parent noun
A **parent** is your mother or your father.
*Both my **parents** came to meet my teacher at Parents' Evening.*

park noun
A **park** is an area of land in a town with grass and trees where people can come for a walk and children can play.
*There is a children's playground in the town **park**.*

parrot noun
A **parrot** is a bird with brightly coloured feathers and a large beak.
*A pet **parrot** can learn to say words and make other noises like whistling!*

party noun
A **party** is when a group of people get together and have fun on a special occasion such as a birthday.
*I had a lovely time at my cousin's **party**.*

pasta noun
Pasta is a food made from flour and water and sometimes egg. It comes in different shapes like macaroni and spaghetti. It is cooked and served with a sauce such as a tomato or cheese sauce.
*I like a spoonful of grated cheese with my **pasta**.*

pat verb
If you **pat** something, you slap it gently with an open hand.
*The little girl loves to **pat** her dog.*

path noun
A **path** is a long narrow strip of ground that goes from one place to another place. People walk or cycle along paths.
*We followed the **path** through the woods.*

paw noun
A **paw** is the name given to the foot of some animals like dogs and bears.
*The dog cut its **paw** on a piece of broken glass.*

pawpaw noun
A **pawpaw** is a fruit with a yellowish-green skin. Its sweet orange flesh can be eaten. **Papaya** is another name for pawpaw.
*Sometimes we have **pawpaw** for breakfast.*

peach noun
A **peach** is a round fruit with a seed stone in the middle and juicy yellow flesh.
*We had **peaches** with our lunch.*

peanut noun
A **peanut** is the seed of a South American plant that is grown in hot countries all over the world. Peanuts are roasted and salted and used as a snack.
***Peanuts** are also made into peanut butter.*

pear noun
A **pear** is a reddish-brown or green fruit with white flesh that can be eaten or made into juice.
*I like eating **pears** and my sister likes eating peaches.*

pea noun
A **pea** is a small green seed that grows inside a pod and is eaten as a vegetable. Peas can be eaten raw or cooked.
*He loves **peas** in his rice.*

pebble noun
A **pebble** is a small smooth stone that is found on beaches and in rivers.
*The children were throwing **pebbles** into the river.*

peg noun
1 A **peg** is a short bit of metal or wood that you attach to a wall or the back of a door to hang things from.
*We hang our towels on **pegs** in the bathroom.*
2 A **peg** can also be a clothes peg, which is a kind of clip made of plastic or wood. You use clothes pegs to hang washing on a washing line.
*My mum out the washing using clothes **pegs**.*

pen noun
1 A **pen** is a long thin tool for writing with ink on paper.
*He wrote a 'thank you' letter using his new **pen**.*
2 A **pen** is also a small place with a fence round it, in which animals are kept.
*They kept a few goats in a **pen** behind their house.*

pencil noun
A **pencil** is a long thin piece of wood or plastic with some black or coloured material inside. You use pencils for writing or drawing.
*She used a **pencil** to draw a picture.*

penguin noun
A **penguin** is a large seabird with a black back and wings and a white front. Penguins cannot fly and use their wings as fins when they are swimming.
***Penguins** are very fast swimmers.*

people noun
1 When we use the word **people**, we are talking about more than one person.
*At least four **people** saw him walking along the street.*
2 **People** can also mean men, women and children.
*His uncle is a nice person and lots of **people** like him.*

pepper noun
1 A **pepper** is a red, yellow or green vegetable that is hollow inside.
***Peppers** can be eaten raw in salads or cooked.*

2 **Pepper** is crushed white or black peppercorns that you sprinkle on food to give it a hot taste.
*She put too much **pepper** on her food and it made her sneeze.*

person noun
A **person** is one man, woman or child.
*He is the tallest **person** in the class.*

pet noun
A **pet** is an animal, such as a cat or a dog, that lives in a house with its owner.
*We have three **pets** – two dogs and a cat!*

phone (telephone) noun
A **phone** is a device that lets two people speak to each other when they are far away from each other.
*My aunt spoke on the **phone** to her friend in America.*

photo (photograph) noun
A **photo** is a picture taken by a camera.
*She took lots of **photos** when she was on holiday.*

piano noun
A **piano** is a large musical instrument. You play a piano by pressing its black and white keys with the fingers of both hands.
*She played a short piece of music on the **piano**.*

picnic noun
A **picnic** is a simple meal eaten outside and away from home.
*We had a **picnic** on the beach.*

picture noun
1 A **picture** is a drawing or a painting of a place or a person.
*The artist painted a **picture** of our house.*
2 A **picture** is also a photo of a place or people.
*She takes lots of **pictures** with her new mobile phone.*

pie noun
A **pie** is a cooked food made with meat or fruit, covered with pastry, and baked in a deep dish.
*Everyone in my family likes apple **pie**.*

piece noun
A **piece** is a small part of something or a bit of something.
*She made a picture using **pieces** of coloured paper.*

pig noun
A **pig** is a farm animal that has a large head with a long nose, a fat body and short legs.
***Pigs** use their long noses to dig into earth to find food.*

pillow noun
You rest your head on a **pillow** when sleeping in your bed.
***Pillows** are filled with soft material like feathers.*

pin noun
A **pin** is a small thin piece of metal with a sharp point at one end and a small round head at the other.
*My mum used **pins** to hold the two pieces of fabric together before sewing them together with a needle and thread.*

pineapple noun
A **pineapple** is a large fruit with sweet yellow flesh and a hard greenish-yellow skin.
***Pineapples** can be eaten fresh or cooked.*

pink noun
If something is **pink**, it is the colour of a flamingo or strawberry ice cream.
*Mix white paint with a little red paint to make the colour **pink**.*

pirate noun
In the olden days, a **pirate** was someone who attacked ships at sea and robbed them of their treasure.
*Her little boy likes to dress up as a **pirate**.*

pizza noun
Pizza is a flat round Italian bread that has tomato and cheese and other things on top and is baked in an oven.
*They got some **pizza** from the takeaway.*

plane (aeroplane) noun
A **plane** is a flying vehicle with wings that is powered by a jet engine or propellers.
***Planes** are used to fly people or cargo from place to place.*

planet noun
A **planet** is a large round object that moves around a star in outer space.
*Earth is a **planet** moving round a star (the sun).*

plant noun
A **plant** is something that grows in the earth. A plant has roots, a stem, flowers, seeds and leaves.
***Plants** need sunshine and water to grow.*

plastic noun
Plastic is a material made in a factory from oil, natural gas, coal or plants. It is easy to shape plastic to make many different solid objects.
*A lot of soft drinks are sold in bottles made of **plastic**.*

plate noun
A **plate** is a round flat dish. We put the food we are going to eat on plates.
*He ate everything on his **plate**.*

platform noun
A **platform** is the part of a railway station next to the railway line. You get on or off a train from the platform.
*Our train was leaving from **Platform** 4.*

play verb
1 When you **play**, you have lots of fun doing something you enjoy.
*The children love to **play** outside in the playground at breaktime.*
2 If you **play** a sport, you take part in that sport.
*I **play** netball at school.*
3 If you **play** an instrument, such as a piano or a guitar, you make that instrument produce musical sounds.
*She is learning to **play** the piano.*

playground noun
A **playground** is a special outdoor place in a school or in a park where children can play.
*There are slides and climbing frames in the **playground**.*

please adverb
Please is a word that you say when you ask for something nicely.
*'**Please** pass me the tomato sauce.'*

pocket noun
A **pocket** is like a small bag that is sewn into some of your clothes.
*He put his bus ticket in the back **pocket** of his jeans.*

polar bear noun
A **polar bear** is a large white bear that lives in the Arctic, mainly on sea ice.
Polar bears are very good swimmers.

police noun
The **police** are the people whose job it is to keep order and catch anyone who breaks the law.
When our car was stolen, my dad called the police.

pond noun
A **pond** is an area of shallow water that is smaller than a lake.
There are some small fish in the pond.

pony noun
A **pony** is a small horse. Ponies often have thicker coats, manes and tails than horses.
They had horses and ponies at the stables.

potato noun
A **potato** is a common white vegetable that grows in the ground. It is often round and is hard with a brown or reddish-brown skin.
She added some potatoes to the curry she was making.

pram noun
A **pram** is like a small bed on four wheels, used to move a baby around. It has a handle and can be pushed along by a person on foot.
She put her baby into his pram and he soon fell asleep.

present noun
A **present** is something nice that someone gives you to keep.
She was given some lovely presents on her birthday.

press verb
If you **press** something, you push it quite hard but not so hard that you make it move away from you.
She pressed the button to put the TV on.

pretty adjective
If someone or something is **pretty**, they are nice to look at.
She was wearing a very pretty necklace.

prince noun
A **prince** is the son of a king or queen.
The prince will become king when his father dies.

princess noun
A **princess** is the daughter of a king or queen. A woman who marries a prince becomes a princess.
The princess had lots of beautiful clothes.

prize noun
A **prize** is something you win or get as a reward for doing something well.
She won first prize in the race.

pudding noun
Pudding is a sweet food eaten at the end of a meal.
They had apple pie for pudding.

puddle noun
A **puddle** is a small pool of rainwater on the ground.
*Her little brother loves jumping in **puddles**.*

pull verb
If you **pull** something, you get hold of it and move it towards you.
*My mum opened the envelope and **pulled** out a letter.*

puppy noun
A **puppy** is a very young dog.
*There were six **puppies** lying in the basket.*

purple adjective
If something is **purple**, it is the colour of lavender flowers and eggplants.
*Amethyst is a **purple** semi-precious stone.*

purse noun
A **purse** is a kind of small bag made of leather or plastic that can be closed. It is used for carrying money.
*The girl had enough money in her **purse** to buy a small present for her mum.*

push verb
1 If you **push** something, you make it move to a different place.
*He **pushed** his bike up the hill.*
2 If you **push** someone, you use your hands to move them away from you.
*She **pushed** people out of her way to get to the front of the line.*

put verb
If you **put** something somewhere, you move it to that place.
*He **put** his clothes in his cupboard.*

puzzle noun
1 A **puzzle** is a game or a problem that you have to work out by thinking very hard.
*My mum helped me to work out the answer to the word **puzzle**.*
2 A **puzzle** is something that is hard to understand or explain.
*I don't know why she is so angry – it's a **puzzle**.*

pyjamas noun
Pyjamas are the loose trousers and matching top that people wear in bed.
*His **pyjamas** have red and white stripes.*

pyramid noun
A **pyramid** is an object that has triangular sides that meet at a point at the top, with a base shaped like a square, a triangle or a rectangle.
*The **pyramids** built in ancient Egypt are made of stone.*

Qq

quack *noun*
A **quack** is the noise made by a duck.
*Our ducks make very loud **quacks** when they get a fright.*

queen *noun*
A **queen** is a woman who rules a country. A woman who is the wife of a king is also called a queen.
*Cleopatra was **queen** of Egypt.*

question *noun*
A **question** is something that you ask that needs an answer.
*'Where are you going?' is a **question**.*

queue *noun*
A **queue** is a line of people, or a line of traffic, waiting for their turn to do something.
*There was a long **queue** of people waiting for the next bus.*

quick *adjective*
If someone or something is **quick**, they are moving very fast.
*He will still catch his train if he is **quick**.*

quiet *adjective*
If someone or something is **quiet**, they are making little or no noise.
*The children were very **quiet** while their teacher was telling them a story.*

Rr

rabbit *noun*
A **rabbit** is a small furry animal with long ears and a short tail. Rabbits have large powerful back legs and live in underground rabbit holes.
*We watched the **rabbits** eating grass in the field.*

race *noun*
A **race** is a competition to see who is the fastest among a group of runners, swimmers, horses or cars.
*My sister likes running in **races** but she has never won a race.*

radio *noun*
A **radio** is a device you use to hear radio programmes.
*My mum likes listening to music on the **radio**.*

railway *noun*
1 A **railway** is the metal track that a train runs on.
*A lot of trains were late because of leaves on the **railway**.*
2 A **railway** is a company or an organisation that has many railway routes. It also has all of the equipment, buildings, trains and people it needs to make them all work well.
*He worked for the **railway** for many years.*

rain noun
Rain is water falling from the sky in small drops.
*It is wet and windy today with lots of **rain** showers.*

rainbow noun
A **rainbow** is an arc or half-circle of seven colours that can sometimes be seen in the sky when the sun is shining and rain is falling at the same time.
*'Look, there's a double **rainbow**!'*

raspberry noun
A **raspberry** is a small soft red fruit that you can eat.
***Raspberries** can be red, black, purple or golden yellow in colour.*

rat noun
A **rat** is an animal like a large mouse, with a long tail and sharp teeth. Rats can carry diseases.
*Baby **rats** are called kittens or pups.*

read verb
When you **read**, you look at and understand written words.
*He likes to **read** books.*

real adjective
1 If something is **real**, it is something that exists. It is something you can touch and see.
*The story was about **real** people and real events.*
2 If something is **real**, it is part of the natural world and has not been made by human beings.
*She thought the flowers were **real** but they were made of paper.*

really adverb
You use **really** to mean very. Really and very are used in front of adjectives or adverbs to make their meaning stronger and more important.
*She is not just a good singer, she is a **really** good singer.*

recipe noun
A **recipe** gives you a list of the food you need to make something like a cake. It also tells you how to make it.

*The **recipe** says you need flour, eggs, butter and sugar to make the cake.*

rectangle noun
A **rectangle** is a shape with four straight sides. It has two long sides opposite each other and two shorter sides opposite each other.
*Most TV screens are the same shape as a **rectangle**.*

recycle verb
When things are **recycled**, they are changed from rubbish (waste) into new materials and objects.
*If you **recycle** paper, it can be used again to make things like egg cartons, paper towels and cardboard.*

red adjective
If something is **red**, it is the colour of a tomato or blood.
*There were green apples and **red** apples for sale on the fruit stall.*

refrigerator see fridge

remember verb
If you **remember** something, you keep it in your mind and do not forget it.
*I **remembered** to brush my teeth before going to bed.*

reptile noun
A **reptile** is a cold-blooded animal whose skin is covered in scales.
*Snakes and crocodiles are **reptiles**.*

rest verb
If you **rest**, you stop what you are doing and sit down or lie down for a time.
*My grandma likes to **rest** in the afternoon.*

reward noun
A **reward** is something you are given for doing something well or for doing something brave.
*She was given some money as a **reward** for working so hard at school.*

rhino (rhinoceros) noun
A **rhino** is a large animal with a thick skin. It has one, or two, horns on its nose and it eats plants.
***Rhinos** are found in Africa and Asia.*

rhyme¹ verb
If a word **rhymes** with another word, it has the same last sound as that word. For example, hand rhymes with land.
*House **rhymes** with mouse. Fat rhymes with cat.*

rhyme² noun
1 A **rhyme** is a word that has the same last sound as another word.
*Top is a **rhyme** for mop and crop.*
2 A **rhyme** is a short poem. In the UK and some other countries, a nursery rhyme is a short poem or song especially for children.
*The little children sat in a circle and sang nursery **rhymes** with their teacher.*

ribbon noun
A **ribbon** is a long narrow piece of coloured material.
*She was wearing a pink **ribbon** in her hair.*

rice noun
Rice is the seed of a kind of grass. It is eaten as a food. Rice is grown in hot countries with lots of rain.
*A lot of people in the world eat **rice** as their main food.*

rich adjective
If someone is **rich**, they have lots of money.
*The **rich** man lived in a very big house.*

ride verb
When you **ride** something, such as a horse or a bike, you sit on it and control how it moves.
*When he **rides** his bike, he moves it along by pushing the pedals round and round with his feet.*

right *adjective*
1 If something is **right**, it is correct, there are no mistakes.
The boy gave the right answer to the teacher's question.
2 Right is used to describe something that is not on the same side of your body as your heart.
She holds a pencil in her right hand when writing.

ring *noun*
1 A **ring** is a piece of jewellery worn on a finger.
Some rings are made of gold.

2 A **ring** is another word for a circle.
The children sat in a ring and listened to a story.

river *noun*
A **river** is a large amount of fresh water that flows through the land and into the sea, a lake or another river.
The Nile is the longest river in the world.

road *noun*
A **road** is like a wide path that goes from place to place. Roads that are used by a lot of vehicles, such as cars and lorries, are made with a hard top layer.
There are roads all over the country, from narrow country roads to large motorways.

robot *noun*
A **robot** is a machine with its own computer. Robots help human beings by doing the kind of jobs that have to be done over and over again.
Robots are used in some car factories.

rock *noun*
A **rock** is a very large stone.
During the earthquake, some rocks fell down the hill onto the road.

rocket *noun*
1 A **rocket** is tall thin round vehicle that is pushed up into space by a very powerful jet engine.
The rocket was launched into space.
2 A **rocket** is also a type of firework that shoots up into the air. Rockets make lots of noise, sparks and smoke.
There were lots of rockets at the fireworks display.

roll *noun*
A **roll** is like a small loaf of bread.
My dad likes a roll with his soup.

roof noun
A **roof** is the top part of a house. It protects the inside of the house from the weather.
*Our **roof** was damaged in the stormy weather.*

room noun
A **room** is one of the inside parts of a building.
*I live in a house with four **rooms**.*

round adjective
If something is **round**, it is the same shape as a ball or a circle.
*The full moon is **round**.*

roundabout noun
A **roundabout** is a kind of device in a play area that is pushed round and round while children sit or stand on it.
*I hold on tight as the **roundabout** goes round and round.*

rubber noun
Rubber is a strong elastic waterproof substance that comes from the milky liquid in some tropical trees.
*The bouncy ball was made of **rubber**.*

rubbish noun
Rubbish is things we have thrown out because they are no longer useful or needed.
*Some **rubbish** can be recycled and used again.*

rucksack noun
A **rucksack** is a large bag with straps that you carry on your back.
*My dad is carrying all the things he needs for his long journey in his **rucksack**.*

rude adjective
If someone is **rude**, they speak in an angry way to other people and hurt their feelings.
*The shop assistant felt very sad after a customer was very **rude** to her.*

rug noun
A **rug** is a small carpet.
*I have a soft **rug** next to my bed.*

ruler noun
A **ruler** is a short straight piece of wood, plastic or metal that you use to draw straight lines or to measure how long, tall or small things are.
*I left my **ruler** at school by mistake.*

run verb
When you **run**, you move more quickly on your feet than you do when you are walking.
*When school is over, she likes to **run** all the way home.*

runway noun
A **runway** is a strip of ground at an airfield used by planes for landing and taking off.
*The plane touched down on the **runway**.*

rush verb
When you **rush** somewhere, you go there very quickly and in a great hurry.
*I **rushed** into the room and bumped into my mother.*

Ss

sad *adjective*
When someone is **sad**, they feel unhappy.
*He was **sad** because no one played with him at school.*

safe *adjective*
1 If someone is **safe** they are all right and not in any danger.
We were glad to hear that everyone was safe after the storm.
2 If something is **safe** to do or to use, there is no risk or danger to people using it or doing it.
*It is not **safe** to talk to strangers.*

salad *noun*
Salad is a mixture of cold foods, such as different kinds of lettuce and other leafy green vegetables, and raw vegetables like tomatoes and carrots.
*At the restaurant, he ordered a large **salad**.*

salt *noun*
Salt is a white powder that comes from rock salt or seawater. Salt is used when cooking or eating food. Salt is also used to de-ice roads in countries that have cold winters.
*Eating too much **salt** is bad for you.*

same *adjective*
If things are the **same**, they are not different in any way.
*We have twin boys in our class that look exactly the **same**.*

sand *noun*
Sand is the tiny pieces of rock and coral and shells (grains) that cover beaches and deserts all over the world.
*We dug a big hole in the **sand** on the beach.*

sandals *noun*
Sandals are light shoes with open toes and straps.
*I love wearing **sandals** when the weather is hot.*

sandwich *noun*
A **sandwich** is two slices of bread with some sort of filling between them.
*I like **sandwiches** made with brown bread.*

sausage *noun*
A **sausage** is a mixture of meat, salt and spices stuffed into a long thin skin.
*My dad cooked the **sausages** on the barbecue.*

saucepan see **pan**

saw *noun*
A **saw** is a hand tool or a machine with a thin metal blade that has a jagged edge. Saws are used for cutting wood and other hard materials.
*My dad used his **saw** to cut up some logs for the fire.*

scarf noun
A **scarf** is a long piece of fabric that you wear round your neck to keep you warm or to make you look nice.
*My aunt was wearing a lovely **scarf** round her neck.*

school noun
A **school** is a place where children go to be educated.
*There are some good teachers at my **school**.*

scissors noun
Scissors are a small hand tool with two sharp parts that are used for cutting things like paper or cloth.

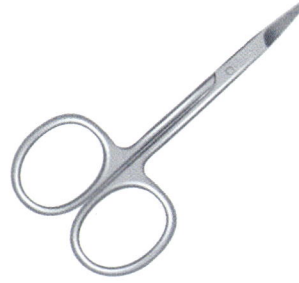

*She cuts her little boy's nails with her nail **scissors**.*

scooter noun
A **scooter** is a child's toy that has a footboard with two wheels and a long steering handle. To make the scooter move, you keep one foot on the footboard and push against the ground with your other foot.
*He fell off his **scooter** and hurt his arm.*

screen noun
1 A **screen** is the big flat surface on which films are shown in a cinema.
*We watched the film on the big **screen**.*
2 A **screen** is also the front surface of a television, computer or smartphone on which images and words are shown.
*His computer has a large **screen**.*

sea noun
The **sea** is all of the salt water that covers much of the earth. All kinds of different creatures live in the sea, from huge killer whales to tiny tropical fish.
*Ships travel all over the world on the **sea**.*

seagull noun
A **seagull** is a common grey or white seabird with black markings on its wings or head. Seagulls have long wings and webbed feet.

*The **seagull** snatched my sandwich before I had time to take a bite!*

seaside noun
The **seaside** is an area close to the sea that includes the beach and places where you can get something to eat.
*People like to go to the **seaside**.*

season noun
A **season** is one of the four parts of the year (spring, summer, autumn and winter).
*In some countries, winter is the **season** for cold weather and snow.*

seat noun
A **seat** is something to sit on that has a back, like a chair.
*There were **seats** for everyone at the meeting.*

see verb
If you **see** something, you use your eyes to look at it.
*I can **see** the sea from my window.*

seesaw noun
A **seesaw** is something for children to play on. It is a long plank of wood balanced so that when one end goes up, the other goes down. A child sits on each end and they take it in turns to push the ground with their feet so that the seesaw goes up and down.
*She loves to play on the **seesaw** with her friend.*

shadow noun
A **shadow** is the dark shape that appears on the ground when someone or something gets in the way of the sun or some other light.
*My big sister's **shadow** is much longer than my shadow because she is taller than me.*

shake verb
If you **shake** something, you move it very quickly up and down or from side to side.
*The baby's toy makes a noise when you **shake** it.*

shape noun
1 The **shape** of something is the way it looks from the outside.
*The little boy's birthday cake is in the **shape** of a football.*
2 Simple **shapes** are the circle, square, triangle and rectangle.
*He coloured in six **shapes**: two circles, two squares and two triangles.*

share verb
If you **share** something, you give part of it to others.
*She **shared** her bar of chocolate with her friends.*

shark noun
A **shark** is a large sea fish with a long body, dull grey skin, very sharp teeth and a pointed fin on its back.
*There are over 500 kinds of **shark** in the oceans of the world.*

sharp adjective
If something is **sharp**, it has a part that is able to cut through things, or it has a point that is able to go into or through something.
*The **sharp** needle went into my finger and made it bleed.*

sharpener noun
A **sharpener** is a small device for sharpening the tip of a pencil so that it can be used for writing or drawing.
*I need a new **sharpener** because my old one does not work anymore.*

shed noun
A **shed** is a small building that is often made of wood. It is usually found in people's back gardens. A shed can be used to store garden tools like lawnmowers and other things.
*They keep their bikes in a **shed**.*

sheep noun
A **sheep** is a farm animal with a heavy woollen coat. Sheep are kept for their meat and their wool.
*Young **sheep** are called lambs.*

shelf noun
A **shelf** is a long flat piece of wood, metal or glass that is fixed to a wall or inside a cupboard.
*I have a **shelf** for my books above my bed.*

shell noun
A **shell** is the hard covering of an egg and a nut. Some sea creatures and some animals also have a hard shell.
*Walnuts have hard **shells**. Tortoises have hard **shells**.*

ship noun
A **ship** is a large boat that carries a lot of things or a lot of people across the sea.
*They are travelling to India by **ship** instead of by plane.*

shirt noun
A **shirt** is a piece of clothing with a collar and buttons that boys and men wear on the top half of their bodies.
*My dad likes to wear a clean **shirt** every day.*

shoe noun
A **shoe** is something you wear on your foot to protect it. A shoe covers your foot but goes no higher than your ankle.
*He has a pair of brown **shoes**.*

shop noun
A **shop** is a place you go to when you want to buy something. Different shops sell different things.
*He went to the shoe **shop** to buy his son some new shoes.*

short adjective
1 If someone is **short**, they are not very tall.
*My brother was quite **short** when he was a young boy but he is much taller now.*
2 If something is **short**, it is not very tall or not very long.
*She has very **short** hair.*

shorts noun
Shorts are short trousers that end at the knee. People wear shorts in hot weather or when they are taking part in sports like football.
*As soon as she got home, she changed out of her school uniform into **shorts** and a T-shirt.*

shout verb
If someone **shouts**, they speak or say something in a very loud voice.
*The music was very loud and I had to **shout** so she could hear what I was saying.*

shower noun
1 A **shower** is a short amount of rain, sleet or snow.
*There were a few rain **showers** this afternoon.*
2 A **shower** is a small place in which you stand under a spray of water to wash yourself.
*There was no bath in the bathroom, only a **shower**.*

shut[1] adjective
If something is **shut**, it is not open. If something is shut, it is closed.
*My bedroom door was **shut**.*

shut[2] verb
If you **shut** something, you close it.
*'Did you **shut** the front door?'*

sick *adjective*
If someone is **sick**, they are not well. They are ill.
*His brother is **sick** and cannot go to school.*

silly *adjective*
If something is **silly**, it is foolish and not clever.
*It was a **silly** idea to go out in the heavy rain without a coat.*

sing *verb*
If you **sing**, you make musical sounds with your voice while using words.
*She wants to **sing** in the school choir.*

sink *noun*
A **sink** is a large container fixed to the wall. It has a water supply, taps, a plughole connected to a drain and a plug to stop water draining away. You wash dishes and clothes in a kitchen sink.
*This **sink** has a special mixer tap.*

sister *noun*
Your **sister** is a girl or a woman who has the same mother and father as you.
*My **sister** can play the piano.*

sit *verb*
When you **sit** down, you lower your bottom onto something, such as a chair, and rest there.
*Our teacher told us to **sit** down.*

size *noun*
Size refers to how big or how small a thing is.
*'What **size** of shoe do you take?'*

skateboard *noun*
A **skateboard** is a narrow piece of flat wood with wheels at both ends. You stand on the board with both feet as it moves along, using one foot every now and then to push the skateboard forward.
*There is a skate park near my home where people can ride their **skateboards**.*

skeleton *noun*
Your **skeleton** is all the bones inside your body.
*You can see the bones that make up your **skeleton** when you are X-rayed.*

skin *noun*
Your **skin** is the thin outside covering of your body or an animal's body.
*His **skin** was covered in red spots.*

skip *verb*
If you **skip**, you move along lightly and quickly as you hop from one foot to the other.
*She **skipped** along the path.*

skipping rope noun
A **skipping rope** is a long piece of rope that you hold (one end in each hand) and keep turning over your head. Each time the rope hits the ground you jump over it.
She was able to skip twenty times before catching her foot in the skipping rope.

skirt noun
A **skirt** is a piece of clothing that fastens around the waist and covers the lower part of the body from the waist to the legs.
She was wearing a pink skirt and leggings.

sky noun
When you look up into the air, the **sky** is the area above the earth that you can see.
The sun was shining and there wasn't a cloud in the sky.

sleep verb
When you **sleep**, you rest your body and your mind with your eyes closed.
Sometimes when I sleep, I have bad dreams.

sleeve noun
A **sleeve** is the part of your clothes that covers your arm.
She was wearing a top with short sleeves.

slide verb
If someone or something **slides**, they move over something very smoothly without stopping.
He watched the crocodile slide down the bank of the river into the water.

slippers noun
Slippers are soft comfortable shoes that you wear indoors.
I change into my slippers as soon as I get home.

slow adjective
If someone or something is **slow**, they do not move quickly. They take a long time to do something.
She is a slow reader but she understands everything she reads.

slug noun
A **slug** is a small black creature with a long slimy body and no legs. A slug is like a snail but it has no shell.
The slugs in the garden have eaten a lot of our plants.

small adjective
If someone or something is **small**, it is little not big.
The kittens were still very small.

smell verb
If you **smell** something, you notice it or discover it using your nose.
'I can smell smoke. Is something on fire?'

snail noun
A **snail** is a small creature with a hard shell. It has no legs and moves very slowly. It has a long slimy body inside its shell.
There are lots of snails in our garden.

snake noun
A **snake** is a long reptile with no legs. Some snakes have a bite that is poisonous. A snake's skin is covered in scales.
*Because a **snake**'s skin becomes stretched as it grows, its old skin falls off to make room for a new layer of skin underneath.*

sneeze verb
When you **sneeze**, air comes out of your nose and your mouth suddenly and without any warning. A sneeze happens because something has tickled the inside part of your nose.
*My friend has a cold and he can't stop **sneezing**.*

snow noun
In some countries, when it is very cold outside, **snow** falls as soft white flakes from clouds in the sky.
*We made a snowman when we had **snow** last winter.*

snowman noun
A **snowman** is a 'man' made of snow. Snow is rolled and packed into shapes, one for his body and a smaller one for his head.
*We put one of my dad's old hats on our **snowman**'s head.*

soap noun
Soap is used with water to wash yourself. You also wash clothes using soap.
***Soap** makes lots of bubbles.*

sock noun
A **sock** is one of two pieces of clothing that we put on our feet before we put on our shoes.
*He has a hole in one of his **socks**.*

sofa noun
A **sofa** is a comfortable seat that two or three people can sit on.
*We have an old leather **sofa**.*

soft adjective
If something is **soft**, it is not hard and changes shape easily when you push down on it.
*My sister likes a **soft** pillow.*

son noun
A **son** is the male child of a mother and father.
*They have two **sons** and a daughter.*

song noun
A **song** is something that you sing. It is a short piece of music with words.
*He wrote the words to the **song** that she was singing.*

sound noun
A **sound** is a noise that you can hear.
*I can hear the **sound** of the wind in the trees.*

soup noun
Soup is a liquid food made by cooking meat or vegetables in water. It is usually eaten when it is hot.
*I had a sandwich and a bowl of pea **soup** for lunch.*

spade noun
A **spade** is a tool with a broad metal blade and a long handle that is used for digging earth.
*My grandpa uses a **spade** to dig up the potatoes in his vegetable plot.*

spaghetti noun
Spaghetti is a type of pasta in the form of long thin strings.
*I love **spaghetti** in a tomato sauce.*

spider noun
A **spider** is a small creature with eight legs. It spins webs to make a nest for itself and to catch insects to eat.
*Some **spiders** can give you a nasty bite.*

spoon noun
A **spoon** has a small bowl at one end and a long handle. We use spoons when cooking and when eating food like soup or custard.
*She remembered to put out **spoons** for everyone to eat their soup.*

spring noun
Spring is the season of the year between winter and summer.
*The weather gets warmer and new leaves start to appear on the trees in **spring**.*

square noun
A **square** is a shape with four straight sides that are the same length.
*The teacher asked her pupils to look for things in the classroom that were the same shape as a **square**, such as a picture frame.*

squeeze verb
If you **squeeze** something soft, you press it hard with your fingers.
*I **squeezed** some oranges to make their juice come out.*

squirrel noun
A **squirrel** is a small reddish-brown or grey animal with a bushy tail that spends most of its time in trees.
*You can see lots of red **squirrels** in parts of Scotland.*

stadium noun
A **stadium** is a large open space with rows of seats all round it where people take part in athletics and play other sports.
*A big football match was being played in the **stadium**.*

stairs noun
Stairs are a set of steps in a building that are used for going up to, and coming down from, the floor or floors above.
*When the lift is not working in our building, we have to use the **stairs**.*

star noun
1 A **star** is a very large object in outer space that is made of burning gas. Stars in the night sky look like very small twinkling lights because they are so far away from earth.
*The nearest **star** to earth is the sun.*
2 A **star** is a shape with five sharp points.
*The teacher put a gold **star** on her pupil's work because it was so good.*

starfish noun
A **starfish** is a small, flat sea creature whose five arms make it look like a star.
*They looked for **starfish** in rock pools at the seaside.*

station noun
A **station** can be a railway station or a bus station. A station is one of the main places where people can get on or off a train or a bus.
*We got to the **station** just in time to catch the bus.*

stay verb
1 If someone **stays** somewhere, they live there all the time.
*I **stay** in a small town in the country.*
2 Sometimes when you **stay** in a place, you only spend a short time there.
*He **stayed** in the city for a few days.*
3 If someone tells you to **stay** where you are or stay how you are, they mean you must not move from that place or change how you are.
*'Stay here and **stay** still, while I go for help.'*

stick¹ noun
A **stick** is a long thin bit of wood or some other material.
*She collected some **sticks** to help make a fire.*

stick² verb
If you **stick** things together, you make them stay together using something like glue.
*He used glue to **stick** bits of coloured paper to his drawing.*

sticker noun
A **sticker** is a small piece of paper with pictures or writing on one side and glue on the other.
*Because she got all her spellings right, the teacher gave the girl a **sticker** that said 'Well Done'.*

sticker book noun
A **sticker book** is a book in which you can use stickers to finish a picture or decorate a page.
*My little sister was given a **sticker** book on her birthday.*

sticky adjective
If something is **sticky**, it is covered in something that sticks to people or things.
*The children's hands were **sticky** after eating some cake.*

stone noun
1 **Stone** is the hard material that rock is made of.
*The houses were made with blocks of **stone**.*
2 A **stone** is a small piece of rock.
*The path was covered in **stones**.*

stop verb
1 If something **stops**, it no longer moves or works.
*Her watch **stopped** during the night.*
2 If someone **stops** doing something, they do not do it anymore.
*He **stopped** smoking cigarettes long ago.*

story noun
A **story** is something you read, or listen to, that tells you about something that has happened. Stories can be true or not true.
*I love it when my mum tells me a **story**.*

straight *adjective*
If something is **straight**, it has no curves or bends.
*My ruler is **straight** and it helps me draw straight lines.*

strawberry *noun*
A **strawberry** is a sweet red fruit that you can eat. Strawberry plants grow on the ground.
***Strawberries** have their seeds on the outside.*

street *noun*
A **street** is a road in a town or a city. Streets have houses or buildings on one side of them, or on both sides, and pavements for people to walk on.
*My aunt and uncle live just across the **street** from us.*

strong *adjective*
If someone is **strong**, they have big muscles and can lift heavy things and do heavy work.
*He is a very **strong** man.*

sugar *noun*
Sugar comes from plants like sugar cane. It is used in food and drinks to make them taste sweet.
*Too much **sugar** is bad for you.*

suitcase see **case**

sum *noun*
1 The **sum** is the total amount you get when you add together two or more numbers.
*12 is the **sum** of 4 + 2 + 6.*

2 Sums is another word for arithmetic problems or number work.
*We did **sums** in class today and I got them all right.*

summer *noun*
Summer is the season of the year between spring and autumn.
*It can get very hot in **summer**.*

sun *noun*
The **sun** is the huge star that gives the earth heat and light. The earth moves round (orbits) the sun. It takes 365 days for the earth to go around the sun once.
*The **sun** rises in the east and sets in the west.*

surprise *noun*
When you get a **surprise**, something happens that you were not expecting. Surprises can be good or bad.
*He got a lovely **surprise** when he saw his dad's new car.*

swan *noun*
A **swan** is a large white water bird with a long neck that feeds in the water and on land.
*Baby **swans** are known as cygnets.*

sweet[1] noun
A **sweet** is a small sweet thing, like a toffee or a chocolate, that is eaten as a treat.
*Don't eat too many **sweets**! They are bad for your teeth.*

sweet[2] adjective
If something tastes **sweet**, it tastes of sugar or honey and is not sour or bitter.
*My mum likes a cup of hot **sweet** tea when she feels tired.*

swim verb
When you **swim**, you move through water using your arms and legs.
*He loves to **swim** when the weather is hot.*

swimming pool noun
A **swimming pool** is a very large container full of water in which people can swim.
*She is learning to swim in a large **swimming pool**.*

swing noun
A **swing** is a seat that hangs from two chains or ropes fixed to a metal frame or the branch of a tree. You sit on the seat and move forwards and backwards.
*I like pushing my little brother on a **swing**.*

sword noun
A **sword** is a weapon with a long thin blade and a handle.
*He plays at being a pirate with his toy **sword**.*

Tt

table noun
A **table** is a piece of furniture with a flat top and four legs.
*We sit at the kitchen **table** to eat our breakfast.*

tablet noun
1 A **tablet** is medicine in the form of a small pill.
*My mum had a very sore head but she took two headache **tablets** and now she feels better.*
2 A **tablet** is a small personal computer with a touchscreen. A tablet is smaller than a laptop but larger than a smartphone.
*She likes to watch films on her **tablet**.*

tadpole noun
A **tadpole** is a small black creature with a round body and a long tail. It lives in water. A tadpole grows into a frog or a toad.
*There were lots of **tadpoles** in the small pond.*

tail noun
A **tail** is the part of an animal at the end of its body. Tails help animals to balance.
*When my dog saw me, his **tail** began to move from side to side.*

tale noun
Tale is another word for a short story.
*Children love listening to **tales** about animals.*

tame adjective
If an animal is **tame**, it is not wild and is not frightened of people.
*Hens are **tame** birds but eagles are wild birds.*

tap noun
A **tap** is a small device fixed to a water pipe. You can turn taps on or off to control the flow of water.
*He turned on the **tap** and filled his bottle with water.*

taxi noun
A **taxi** is a car with a driver. Taxi drivers will take you where you want to go if you pay them.
*My dad went to the airport in a **taxi**.*

tea noun
Tea is a drink made by pouring boiling water onto the dried leaves of the tea plant.
*I like milk in my **tea**.*

teach verb
If you **teach** someone, you help them to learn about things and show them how to do things.
*Her dad is going to **teach** her how to swim.*

teacher noun
A **teacher** is a person whose job it is to help others to learn.
*My friend's mum is a **teacher** at my school.*

team noun
1 A **team** of people is a group of people who work together.
*The firemen worked as a **team** to put out the fire.*
2 A **team** is a group of people who play for the same side in a sport like football.
*She has been chosen to play for the school netball **team**.*

teddy (teddy bear) noun
A **teddy** is a child's soft toy that looks like a small bear.
*The little girl took her **teddy** to bed with her every night.*

telephone see **phone**

television see **TV**

tennis noun
Tennis is a ball game played by two or four players. Tennis players use a kind of bat called a racket to hit the ball to each other over a net.
*If you want to be good at **tennis**, you need to be quick on your feet.*

tent noun
A **tent** is a place that gives you somewhere to stay for a short time. It is made of cloth, with poles to hold it up and pegs or ropes fixed into the ground to stop it blowing away.

*The hurricane damaged a lot of homes and people had to live in **tents** for months.*

thank verb
When you **thank** someone, you are saying to them that it was very nice of them to do something for you or to give you something.
*The teacher **thanked** her pupils for behaving so well on their school outing.*

throw verb
If you **throw** something, you send whatever you are holding flying into the air with a sudden movement of your arm.
*He can **throw** a ball very far when he is playing cricket.*

thumb noun
Your **thumb** is the short thick finger on one side of your hand that is lower than your other fingers. Thumbs help you to grip things.
*My dad hit his **thumb** with a hammer when he was putting a nail in the wall.*

thunder noun
Thunder is the loud sound in the sky that you hear after a flash of lightning.
*Our dog doesn't like the noise made by **thunder** during a storm.*

ticket noun
A **ticket** is a small piece of paper or card that you are given when you pay to travel on a plane, train or a bus. You also need a ticket to get into places like the cinema or a football match.
*We have **tickets** for the cinema this weekend.*

tickle verb
When you **tickle** someone, you move your fingers gently and quickly on part of their body to make them laugh.
*She **tickled** the baby under his arm and he began to laugh.*

tidy adjective
If a room is **tidy**, it is clean and everything is in its place. There is no mess or stuff left lying around.
*We try to keep our classroom clean and **tidy**.*

tiger noun
A **tiger** is a very large wild cat. Tigers are found in Asia. They have orange-coloured coats with black stripes.
*The **tiger** is the largest member of the cat family.*

tight adjective
If something is **tight**, it is not loose. If clothes are tight, they stick very close to your body.
*Her new shoes were very **tight** and she soon had a sore bit called a blister on her heel.*

tights noun
Tights are a type of tight, thin clothing worn mainly by girls and women. Tights cover your feet, legs and hips.
*Her **tights** have a hole in them.*

time noun
Time is any moment in the day that we talk about in terms of hours and minutes after midnight (am) or after midday (pm).
*'What's the **time**?'*
'Right now, the time is ten minutes past three (hours) in the afternoon, or 3.10 pm.'

tiny *adjective*
If something is **tiny**, it is very small.
*There were a lot of **tiny** insects in the grass.*

toast *noun*
A slice of **toast** is a slice of bread that has been burned a little in a toaster or under a grill.
*She loves **toast** and peanut butter for breakfast.*

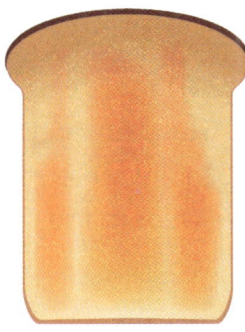

today *noun*
Today is this day, here and now, and not yesterday or tomorrow.
*There is no rain **today** – it is sunny.*

toe *noun*
A **toe** is one of the five parts at the end of each foot.
*I dropped a book on my big **toe**!*

tomato *noun*
A **tomato** is a soft round red fruit that is eaten as a vegetable. You can eat tomatoes raw in salads or cooked in sauces.
*My dad used **tomatoes** to make a sauce for the pasta.*

tongue *noun*
Your **tongue** is the thick, soft part that moves inside your mouth when you are speaking or eating. Your tongue helps you to talk and to taste your food.
*The soup was hot and it burned my **tongue**.*

tool *noun*
A **tool** is a thing you need to do some jobs. Most tools are held in the hand.
*A hammer is a **tool**.*

tooth *noun*
A **tooth** is one of the small hard white objects that grow in the top and bottom of your mouth. You use your teeth to bite and chew your food.
*When I had a sore **tooth**, my parents took me to see a dentist.*

toothbrush *noun*
A **toothbrush** is a small brush that you use to clean your teeth.
*She uses a **toothbrush** and toothpaste to clean her teeth in the morning and at night.*

top *noun*
1 The **top** of something is the place where it is highest.
*He walked up to the **top** of the mountain.*
2 A **top** is a piece of clothing, such as a shirt or a jumper, that you wear on the top part of your body.
*Her mum got her a new **top** at the shops.*

tortoise *noun*
A **tortoise** is a reptile that lives on land. It has four legs and a large hard shell on top of its body.
***Tortoises** live longer than any other land animal in the world.*

touch *verb*
1 If you **touch** someone or something, you place your hand on them and take it away quickly.
*She **touched** the wall to see if the paint was dry.*
2 If something **touches** something, it comes up against it, leaving no space between the two things.
*The car **touched** the cyclist and knocked him off his bike.*

towel noun
A **towel** is a piece of soft fabric that we use to dry ourselves.
*She dried herself with a **towel** after her shower.*

tower noun
A **tower** is a tall narrow building or a part of a building such as a church or a castle.
*There was a flag flying from the castle **tower**.*

town noun
A **town** is a place that is smaller than a city but larger than a village. It has houses and other buildings and streets.
*We live in a small **town** near the sea.*

toy noun
A **toy** is something that a child plays with such as a doll or a toy animal.
*The little boy's favourite **toy** is his metal truck.*

tractor noun
A **tractor** is a farm vehicle with two large back wheels. A tractor is used to pull things like trailers and ploughs.

*The **tractor** pulled the car out of the mud.*

traditional adjective
If you do something the **traditional** way, you do it in a way that has been passed down from one person to another for many years.
*He likes to make bread the **traditional** way.*

traffic noun
Traffic is all of the vehicles that are moving in an area like a town.
*There was heavy **traffic** along the main road through the town.*

train noun
A **train** is a line of carriages or trucks pulled along a railway track by an engine.
*We went to the city by **train**.*

trainers noun
Trainers are light shoes that you can wear for running and some other sports, or you can wear them every day.
*He puts on his **trainers** after he comes home from school.*

treasure noun
Treasure is a collection of things that are valuable, such as gold coins, silver and jewels.
*Pirates used to bury their **treasure** in secret places.*

tree noun
A **tree** is a very large woody plant with a thick trunk, branches and leaves.
*Wood comes from **trees**.*

triangle noun
1 A **triangle** is a shape that has three straight sides.
*The children were asked to draw, and colour-in, a **triangle**.*
2 A **triangle** is a kind of small musical instrument, made from a piece of metal in the shape of a triangle, that you hit with a metal bar to make a musical sound.
*She plays the **triangle** when the class has a music lesson.*

trousers noun
Trousers are a piece of clothing. Trousers cover you from your waist to your ankles. They have one part for each leg.
*He needs a new pair of **trousers**.*

truck noun
A **truck** is a large heavy road vehicle for carrying goods.
*A lot of noisy **trucks** go through our town.*

try verb
If you **try** to do something, you do your best to get it done.
*He did **try** to lift the box but it was too heavy.*

T-shirt noun
A **T-shirt** is a kind of shirt with short sleeves and no collar.
*She likes to wear a **T-shirt** and shorts when the weather is hot.*

tummy noun
Your **tummy** is your stomach, which is the front part of your body above your legs.
*She had a sore **tummy** and didn't go to school.*

tune noun
A **tune** is a set of musical notes played one after the other to make a pleasant sound.
*I do not know the words of the song but I like the **tune**.*

tunnel noun
A **tunnel** is a long hole that cuts into and under the ground. We build tunnels to go through mountains or under rivers that get in the way of a road or a railway line.
*The road went through a long **tunnel** under the mountain.*

TV (television) noun
A **TV** is an electronic device with a screen on which you can watch programmes and films.
*He loves watching football on the **TV**.*

twins noun
Twins are two children who are born at the same time to the same mother. Some twins look exactly the same – they are called identical twins.
*There are two sets of **twins** in my family.*

twinkle verb
If something **twinkles**, it shines with a small bright light that keeps changing from bright to dim and back again.
*The stars **twinkled** in the night sky.*

Uu

ugly *adjective*
If something is **ugly**, it does not look nice.
*The old block of flats is an **ugly** building.*

umbrella *noun*
An **umbrella** keeps us dry when it is raining. An umbrella is a device with a long handle and a piece of plastic or fabric that is stretched over a folding metal frame.
*When it started to rain heavily, my dad put up his large **umbrella**.*

uncle *noun*
Your **uncle** is the brother of your mother or your father. Your uncle can also be your aunt's husband.
*If you are a boy, you are your **uncle**'s nephew. If you are a girl, you are your uncle's niece.*

undress *verb*
When you **undress**, you take your clothes off.
*She **undressed** before having a bath.*

unicorn *noun*
A **unicorn** is not a real animal. In stories, a unicorn is a magical animal that looks like a white horse with a long mane and tail and a straight horn coming out of the middle of its forehead.
*She loves her toy **unicorn**.*

uniform *noun*
A **uniform** is a set of clothes that all the people in a group wear. For example, soldiers, nurses and schoolchildren all wear uniforms.
*My school **uniform** is grey and blue.*

up *adverb*
If something goes **up**, it moves towards a higher place.
*'Put your hands **up** if you know the answer,' said the teacher.*

upside down *adverb*
If something is **upside down**, the top part is where the bottom part usually is.
*She turned the bottle of honey **upside down** to squeeze out the last of the honey.*

upstairs *adverb*
If you go **upstairs**, you go up the stairs to the higher part of a house or building.
*He ran **upstairs** to his classroom.*

Vv

van noun
A **van** is a vehicle that is smaller than a lorry but bigger than a car. It has no side windows and is used for carrying things from place to place.
*My uncle drives a white **van**.*

vase noun
A **vase** is a container made of glass or china that you put flowers in.
*She put some flowers in a **vase** of water.*

vegetable noun
A **vegetable** is a plant, or part of a plant, that can be eaten raw or cooked.
*You can grow **vegetables**, such as beans and peas, even if you only have a little bit of land.*

vehicle noun
A **vehicle** is a kind of machine, such as a car or a lorry, with wheels and an engine. Vehicles carry people and things from place to place by road.
*A long line of **vehicles** was waiting at the traffic lights.*

very adverb
Very is a word used to make an adjective or an adverb stronger and more important.
*It is **very** hot during a heatwave.*

vest noun
A **vest** is piece of clothing that you wear on your top half under other clothes such as a shirt.
*My mum says I must wear a **vest** in winter to keep me warm.*

vet noun
A **vet** is an animal doctor. He looks after sick or hurt animals.
*When our dog is sick, we take him to the **vet**.*

violin noun
A **violin** is a wooden musical instrument with four strings. You hold a violin under your chin and use a bow to play it. (A bow is a long thin piece of wood with hair from a horse's tail stretched tightly from one end to the other.)
*Someone who plays the **violin** is called a violinist.*

visitor noun
A **visitor** is someone who comes to see a place or a person for a short time.
*The town is full of **visitors** in the holidays.*

volcano noun
A **volcano** is a mountain with an opening at the top, out of which hot liquid rock (lava), gas and dust escape.
*There was a lot of lava running down the side of the **volcano**.*

wake verb
If you **wake** someone, you stop them from sleeping.
*Every morning my mum has to **wake** me up.*

walk verb
If you **walk** somewhere, you get there by moving along on your feet, putting one leg at a time in front of the other. Walking is slower than running.
*Some children have to **walk** a long way to reach their school.*

wall noun
1 A **wall** is made of stones and bricks. It is used to divide up a piece of land or to go round a piece of land.
*There was a **wall** round the house and its garden.*
2 A **wall** is also one side of a room.
*There are some pictures on one of the **walls** in my classroom.*

wand noun
A **wand** is a thin stick that is used to make something magic happen.
*Fairies and magicians use **wands**.*

want verb
If you **want** something, you feel you must have it.
*She was hungry and she **wanted** something to eat.*

warm adjective
If something is **warm**, it feels hot but not very hot.
*I used a hot-water bottle to make my bed **warm**.*

wash verb
When you **wash** something, you use soap and water to make it clean.
*I **washed** myself in the shower.*

wasp noun
A **wasp** is a flying insect with black and yellow stripes. Female wasps can give you a very sore sting.
*Look out! There's a **wasp** in the room!*

waste noun
Waste is things that are not wanted anymore and things that are broken and cannot be used anymore.
*Many places try to recycle their **waste** so that it can be used again in some other way.*

watch¹ noun
A **watch** is like a small clock that you wear on your wrist.
*My **watch** says it is 3 o'clock.*

watch² verb
If you **watch** something, you look at it for quite a long time.
*He **watched** his brother playing football.*

84

water noun
Water is the clear liquid that falls from the clouds as rain. It forms seas, lakes and rivers. People, animals and plants would die without water.
*Lots of people in the world have not got safe clean **water** to drink.*

wave[1] verb
When you **wave**, you lift your hand and move it from side to side.
*We **waved** to my aunt as her train left the station.*

wave[2] noun
A **wave** is a long line of water on top of the sea that curls over before it reaches the shore.
*We enjoyed jumping over the small **waves** as they came in towards the shore.*

web noun
A **web** is made by a spider. It is like a fine net with very thin threads.
*Lots of flies were stuck in the spider's **web**.*

website noun
A **website** is a place on the internet where you can get information about something.
*My mum looked on the school **website** for some information about the school holidays.*

week noun
A **week** is made up of the seven days from Monday to Sunday: Monday, Tuesday, Wednesday, Thursday, Friday, Saturday and Sunday.
*It is the last **week** of our school holidays.*

weekend noun
A **weekend** is the two days at the end of the week when most people are not working (Saturday and Sunday).
*We are going to visit my grandparents this **weekend**.*

well[1] adjective
If you are **well**, you are not sick. When you are well, you are free from illness.
'How are you?'
*'I am very **well**, thank you.'*

well[2] adverb
If you do something **well**, you do it in a good or correct way.
*He plays the piano **well**.*

wellingtons (wellington boots, wellies) noun
Wellingtons are long rubber boots that come up to your knees. You wear wellingtons to keep your feet dry when the ground is wet or muddy.

*My little sister loves jumping in puddles in her **wellingtons**.*

wet adjective
If something is **wet**, it is covered in water or some other liquid.
*The dogs were very **wet** after running about in the rain.*

whale noun
A **whale** is a very large sea mammal with flippers. It breathes through a hole on the top of its head.
*We were very lucky to see **whales** on our boat trip.*

wheel noun
A **wheel** is something round that turns round and round. Wheels are fixed under a car or some other objects to let them move easily over the ground.
*My dad has a desk chair on **wheels** in his office.*

wheelchair noun
A **wheelchair** is a special kind of chair on wheels. You use a wheelchair to get about if you are not able to walk.
*Some **wheelchairs** have electric motors.*

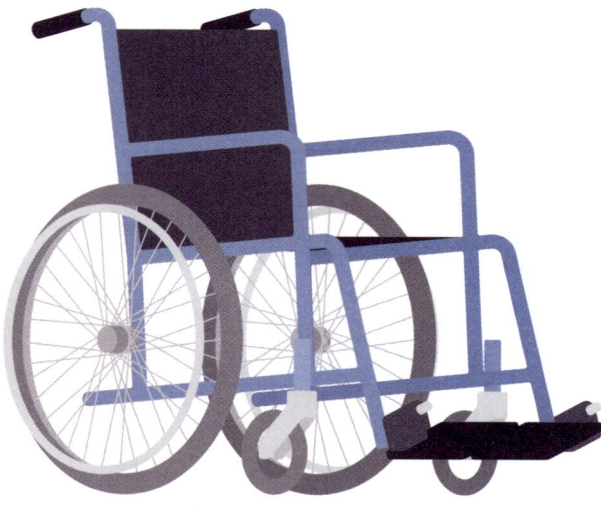

whisper verb
When you **whisper**, you speak very quietly.
*The two naughty children **whispered** to each other in class.*

whistle verb
When you **whistle**, you make a high musical sound by passing air through your teeth or through a hole formed by your lips.
*I have just learned how to **whistle**.*

white adjective
If something is **white**, it is the colour of snow.
*My mum bought me some **white** socks.*

whiteboard noun
A **whiteboard** is a white plastic board that you can write on. It can be wiped clean and is used by teachers and people giving a talk.
*Our teacher wrote some new words on the **whiteboard** for us to learn.*

win verb
If you **win** something, it means you have come first in something like a race.
*I wanted to **win** the race but I tripped and was nearly last!*

wind noun
Wind is air moving quickly across land and sea.
*There was a very strong **wind** and some trees were blown down.*

windfarm noun
A **windfarm** is a place with a lot of wind turbines (machines that use the wind to make electricity).
*The **windfarm** was built on the hillside.*

windmill noun
A **windmill** is a building with four large sails on the outside that turn when the wind is blowing. As the sails turn, they make a machine inside the windmill crush grain to make flour.
*The flour was made in a traditional way in a **windmill**.*

window noun
A **window** is an opening fitted with glass in the walls of a building. Windows let in light. When they are open, they let in fresh air.
*It was such a hot day that all the **windows** in the house were open.*

windy adjective
If it is **windy**, the wind is stronger than usual and blowing a lot.
*It is **windy** and wet today because of the stormy weather.*

wing noun
A **wing** is one of the two parts of a bird's body that it uses to fly.
*Birds, planes and some insects have different kinds of **wings**.*

winter noun
Winter is the season of the year between autumn and spring.
*The **weather** is colder in winter.*

witch noun
A **witch** in stories is usually a bad woman who is able to do magic using spells.
*The **witch** turned the prince into a frog with one of her spells.*

wizard noun
A **wizard** in stories is a man who is able to do magic.
***Wizards** use spells and wands to do their magic.*

woman noun
A **woman** is a grown-up female human being.
*My aunt is a married **woman** with young children.*

wolf noun
A **wolf** is a wild animal and the largest member of the dog family.
*A **wolf** lives with other wolves in groups called packs.*

wood noun
1 A **wood** is a large group of trees growing close to each other.
*It is easy to get lost in a **wood**.*
2 **Wood** is the material that trees are made of. Wood is used to make furniture and other things.
*Our front door is made of **wood**.*

word noun
A **word** is a group of sounds that mean something when you hear them spoken together by a human being. Words can also be written down for people to read.
*The children were learning new **words** every day.*

world noun
The **world** is the planet we live on. It is the earth and all its countries, peoples, animals and plants.
*We all need to take good care of our **world**.*

worm noun
A **worm** is a small animal that has a long thin body with no bones and no arms or legs.
Worms live in the soil under the ground and they help to keep the soil healthy.

Xx

X-ray noun
An **X-ray** is a photo that shows what the inside of your body looks like.
You can see on the X-ray where my ankle bone is broken.

xylophone noun
A **xylophone** is a musical instrument with a row of wooden bars. You play a xylophone by hitting the bars with two small wooden hammers.
She can play a tune on her xylophone.

write verb
When you **write** something, you draw the letters of words with a pen or pencil on paper so that people can read them.
The children were asked to write their names on their notebooks.

wrist noun
Your **wrist** is the joint between your hand and your forearm.
I wear a watch on my wrist.

wrong adjective
1 If something is **wrong**, it is not correct.
They sent my aunt's parcel to the wrong address – it went to someone else's house instead of our house.
2 If there is something **wrong** with something, it is not working properly.
There was something wrong with our car so my sister took it to the garage to be fixed.

Yy

yacht noun
A **yacht** is a type of boat, usually with sails and sometimes with an engine.
*Some **yachts** are big enough to sail around the world.*

year noun
A **year** is a length of time made up of 12 months, or 52 weeks, or 365 days.
*You have a birthday every **year**.*

yellow adjective
If something is **yellow**, it is the colour of the sun in drawings. It is also the colour of a ripe lemon and the petals of a sunflower.
*She was wearing her favourite **yellow** dress.*

yes
1 You say **yes** when someone asks you if you have done something and you have done it.
'Have you fed the dog?'
*'**Yes**, I've fed the dog.'*
2 You say **yes** in answer to a question if you agree with the person asking the question.
'Do you think it is going to rain?'
*'**Yes**, I do.'*
3 You say **yes** in answer to a question if you want to do what the person asking the question wants to do.
'Do you want to play a new game?'
*'**Yes**, I would.'*
4 You say **yes** in answer to a question if you want what the person asking the question is offering you.
'Do you want a chocolate?'
*'**Yes**, please!'*

yesterday noun
Yesterday was the day before today.
***Yesterday** I went swimming and today I am tired.*

yogurt (yoghurt) noun
Yogurt is a slightly sour thick liquid food made from milk. Sometimes it is sweetened or flavoured with fruit.
*She likes **yogurt** and honey for breakfast.*

young adjective
If someone or something is **young**, they are not old. They are in the early part of their life.
*We got our dog when she was quite **young**.*

yo-yo noun
A **yo-yo** is a small round toy at the end of a long piece of string. You can make the yo-yo go up and down using the string.
*She can do lots of tricks with her **yo-yo**.*

Zz

zebra noun
A **zebra** is a wild African animal that belongs to the horse family. Zebras have white coats with black or brown stripes and they eat grass.
Zebras live in small family groups that sometimes get together to make large herds.

zero noun
1 Zero is the number 0.
Someone has left off a zero! There are 300 people coming to the concert, not 30.
2 Zero means not any, nothing.
His chances of winning the spelling competition were zero.

zip noun
A **zip** is a device for holding the two sides of something together.
She closed the zip on her pencil case.

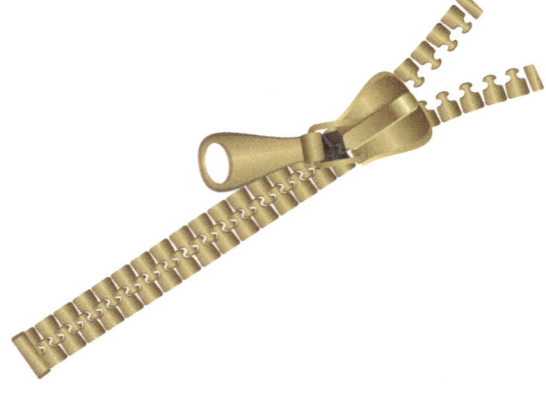

zebra crossing noun
A **zebra crossing** is made up of a strip of black and white stripes painted across a road. Vehicles must stop at a zebra crossing so that people can cross the road safely.
There is a zebra crossing on the busy road near our school.

zoo noun
A **zoo** is a place where wild animals are kept so that people can come and look at them.
China has given some of their panda bears to zoos in other parts of the world.

zoom verb
If something **zooms**, it moves very quickly.
A white car zoomed past.